CONDUCTING
SURVEY RESEARCH
IN THE
SOCIAL SCIENCES

D1519402

Isadore Newman
Keith McNeil

University Press of America,® Inc.
Lanham • New York • Oxford

Copyright © 1998
University Press of America,® Inc.
4720 Boston Way
Lanham, Maryland 20706

12 Hid's Copse Rd.
Cummor Hill, Oxford OX2 9JJ

Library of Congress Cataloging-in-Publication Data

Newman, Isadore.
Conducting survey research in the social science / Isadore Newman,
Keith McNeil
p.   cm.
Includes bibliographical references and index.
l. Social surveys.   I. McNeil, Keith A. II. Title
HN29.N46 1998   300'.7'23—dc21   98-34837 CIP

ISBN 0-7618-1227-X (pbk: alk. ppr.)

Contents

LIST OF FIGURES

LIST OF TABLES

LIST OF EXHIBITS

Preface

The purpose of this text is to present basic concepts and general guidelines for those who are interested in conducting a survey. It is intended to help the reader initiate and develop a survey by outlining the appropriate sequential steps essential to the development of an adequate and useful instrument.

Survey research is generally used to gather information about some defined population by studying a selected sample from that population of interest. These samples are generally studied to discover such things as: incidence of positive or negative opinions on issues held by a particular population, the distribution of those opinions, and the relationship of certain sociological or psychological information to those opinions.

Below are the eight steps of survey research on which this text will focus. Each step has an entire chapter devoted to it. References for further reading can be found at the end of each chapter. The reader will find major questions in each chapter that must be answered. Once those questions are answered, one has a plan for how to conduct the survey to answer the research questions. Three fictitious vignettes are included to illustrate how decisions are made. These vignettes are from three different content areas, illustrating that survey research, though complex, can be conducted to meet many different needs.

The eight steps in conducting survey research are as follows:

Step I.   Specify the Intent of the Survey

Step II.   Assess the Available Resources

Step III.   Define the Population

Step IV.   Review the Pertinent Literature

Step V.   Determine the Data Collection Technique

Step VI.   Develop the Survey

Step VII.   Determine the Sampling Procedure

Step VIII.   Analyze the Results and Prepare the Research Report

Acknowledgements

We would like to thank two students who provided final editing on this text: Michelle Dorsey and Karen Stevens. We would also like to thank the following authors for giving us permission to use some of their material:

William Wilkinson and Keith McNeil for use of their Figure 6.5, which originally appeared in their text, *Research for the helping professions* published in 1997 by Brooks/Cole.

Carolyn R. Benz and J. M. Hudgins for the use of their material originally presented in a paper entitled "Questionnaire Formats" at the Mid-Western Educational Research Association meeting in Chicago in 1990.

Michael T. Oravecz, Frank B. Thomas, and Isadore Newman for material originally presented in a paper entitled, "Sample size as a function of several variables" at the annual meeting of the Mid-Western Educational Research Association, Kansas City, MO in 1980.

Chapter 1

Specify the Intent of the Survey

One does not develop a survey in a vacuum. There is always a purpose for that survey–the purpose depending on the audience wanting the information. Therefore, the audience must be involved in the planning of the survey to make sure that the survey meets their needs.

The term "stakeholders" is associated with those needing the information, and often there are various stakeholders in any one survey. For the survey to be of maximum value (and in some cases of any value), these stakeholders must be involved in deciding the intent of the survey. Exhibits 1, 2, and 3 depict three situations that will be followed throughout the remainder of this text.

Exhibit 1. Analysis of Whom the Stakeholders Are–Psychologist's Needs Assessment Survey

A licensed psychologist has moved into a new community and decides to find out what kinds of problems are not being met by the existing counseling services. He plans to use this information to focus his area of specialization, tailor his advertisements, and possibly decide his hours of service.

Here, the only stakeholder is the psychologist himself. He is obtaining this information for his purposes and his purposes alone.

A face to face meeting should occur between the individual developing the survey and the stakeholders. The stakeholders will usually assume that the survey developer will implicitly be aware of the intent of the survey. Though this may be true sometimes, often such a meeting will reveal additional areas or items that should be on the survey. How the survey should be conducted (Chapter 5), what should be on the survey (Chapter 6), and who should respond to the survey (Chapter 7) can also be clarified by the stakeholders.

If the researcher is the only stakeholder, then it is a good idea to share thoughts and the survey with others knowledgeable in the field. Two heads are always better than one, and the second person, being less ego-involved, can often find errors in assumptions, omissions, or planned data collection.

Try to find a friend to review your survey intent. Better yet, try to find an enemy (or at least an impartial person) to respond to your ideas. Initial clarity will go a long way to producing valuable information.

Exhibit 2. Analysis of Whom the Stakeholders Are–Curriculum Evaluation Survey

The superintendent of School District #101 has been convinced by the sixth-grade teachers that the current math curriculum (from now on called the Old Curriculum) is not effective. After a review of what other nearby districts were using, District #101 decided to pilot the New Curriculum with a few teachers. One evaluation component is a survey of the teachers. Who would be the stakeholders in this scenario? The superintendent is clearly one stakeholder, but the school board, the parents, and all sixth-grade teachers (and probably seventh-grade as well) are other stakeholders. Therefore the survey developer should meet with each of these stakeholders, probably at different times so that the concerns and interests of each group can be shared openly. It is a given that this survey will be addressed to the sixth-grade teachers, but the various stakeholders may have some good suggestions with respect to specific items that should be on the survey.

One might even develop some example tables and figures to show the kind of information that will be obtained and how it will be displayed. When stakeholders see such tables and figures, additional requests are often made, such as reporting the results by gender or school. Forcing stakeholders to consider summarized data before administering the survey can often improve the utility of the survey.

Exhibit 3. Analysis of Whom the Stakeholders Are–Administrative School Uniform Survey

A student working on her doctorate is interested in identifying the opinions of all superintendents regarding the requirement of students wearing school uniforms. She will need to discuss the study with the state organization to get their approval and the mailing list. This meeting can also provide insight into the kinds of questions that should be asked, and any "political" issues that should either be included or excluded. The table shell developed by the researcher is in

Table 1.

One result of the meeting between the doctoral student and the state organization was that the organization's board of directors wanted all superintendents to be surveyed–a census taken on the issue. The board also requested that one item be omitted as the item seemed to them to be contentious and did not fit in with the other items; that item was item 5– "School uniforms are just another educational fad."

The board also requested that the area of academic achievement be addressed, but left the specific item development to the researcher. In fact, they felt that academic achievement was the most important item.

Finally, the board also showed an interest in what the data would look like when broken down into rural and urban categories. It became clear to the researcher that the variable of rural-urban was a piece of information that had to be included on the survey.

Table 1

Example of Table Shell for the School Uniform Survey

	%Yes	% No
1. School uniforms will improve school morale.		
2. School uniforms will be met with resistance from some parents.		
3. School uniforms will decrease absenteeism.		
4. School uniforms will decrease membership in student organizations.		
5. School uniforms will improve academic performance.		

Intent Questions to Answer

Each survey is conducted to find out specific information. However, the usefulness of the information collected is contingent upon how clearly the objectives are stated. These objectives must reflect the purpose of the survey and act as a guide to the development or choice of the survey. Each survey researcher must answer the following questions:

Question 1. What are the basic questions I want my survey to answer?

Question 2. How do I plan to use the information?

Question 3. Who do I plan to survey to obtain those answers?

Question 1. What are the basic questions I want my survey to answer?

Their real problem was that they assumed themselves able to formulate the questions, and ignored the fact that the questions were every bit as important as the answers.   **Robert Ornste**

The formulation of a problem is far more often essential than its solution, which may be merely a matter of mathematical or experimental skill. To raise new questions, new possibilities, to regard old problems from a new angle requires creative imagination and marks real advance in science.
                              A. Einstein and L. Infield

The purpose of the psychologist's survey was to identify the counseling needs so that he could target his services. He was interested in identifying the differences between what people needed and what was available to them. The term used for this kind of survey is "Needs Assessment."

The curriculum survey was designed to decide the utility of the New Curriculum, to help make an informed decision about whether to use the New Curriculum district-wide. The term used for this kind of survey is "Evaluation."

The administrative survey was designed to measure the attitudes and opinions of superintendents. Such an instrument is often called an "Attitude Survey" or "Attitude Questionnaire."

Question 2. How do I plan to use the information?

Let your advance worrying become advanced thinking and planning.
                              Winston Churchill

The psychologist is obtaining the information so that he can make decisions regarding his services. First, are there enough potential clients in the new community to support his specialty? Second, what information (advertising) would lead clients to his service? The third question relates to optimum hours of service. He will use all of this information to plan his clinical office in his new community.

The curriculum evaluator is obtaining information to assist her in deciding whether to adopt the New Curriculum district-wide. The survey of teachers' opinions may be only one piece of information–along with student performance and cost of the two curricula.

The administration doctoral student is obtaining survey information, not to make decisions, but to inform various stakeholders about the opinions of all the superintendents in the state. Such information is usually called basic research since there is no actual decision intended. Various stakeholders might interpret the information differently. For instance, given that 80% of the superintendents favor school uniforms, one superintendent may decide to carry out a school uniform policy. Another superintendent might interpret the results of 80% as not all superintendents favoring school uniforms and therefore refrain from setting up a school uniform policy.

Question 3. Who do I plan to survey to obtain those answers?

Science is simply common sense at its best-that is-rigidly accurate in observation, and merciless to fallacy in logic.   **Thomas H. Huxley**

The psychologist does not have enough time nor money to survey all potential clients in his new community. Indeed, all potential clients cannot be identified. Furthermore, he only needs to survey enough to get some notions about the trends–particularly since he knows he can change his focus without too much trouble or expense.

The administrative survey will be sent to all superintendents as that is the group of interest. Obviously other stakeholders have interests in school uniforms, but often any one survey obtains only one group's viewpoint on an issue.

The curriculum evaluation will be directed to those sixth-grade teachers who used the New Curriculum and those who continued to use the Old Curriculum. As in the above example, there are other stakeholders who have an interest in the evaluation of the New Curriculum, but this survey will be limited to the two groups of teachers. Responses to the three "intent of the survey" questions are summarized in Exhibit 4.

Exhibit 4

Summary of Answers to the "Intent of the Survey" Questions

Question 1. What are the basic questions I want my survey to answer?
    Psychologist-Needs Assessment.
    Administration-Attitude.
    Curriculum-Evaluation.

Question 2. How do I plan to use the information?
    Psychologist-Obtain additional data for personal decisions.
    Administrator-Basic research.
      -Increase knowledgebase.
      -Inform various stakeholders.
    Curriculum evaluator-Choose between competing curricula.

Question 3. Who do I plan to survey to obtain those answers?
Psychologist-A "sample" of all potential clients.
Administration-All superintendents (a "census").
Curriculum-All teachers who used the New Curriculum and also some who used the Old Curriculum.

Additional Reading

Question 1. What are the basic questions I want my survey to answer?

Alreck, P. L., & Settle, R. B. (1985). *The survey research handbook.* Homewood, IL: R. D. Irwin.
Chapter 1 contains a discussion of "why surveys are conducted."

Isaac, S., & Michael, W. B. (1981). Handbook in research and evaluation (2nd ed.). San Diego, CA: EdITS.
Chapter 1 is dedicated to planning for evaluation studies (including needs assessment) and Chapter 2 is dedicated to planning for research studies.

Question 3. Who do I plan to survey to obtain those answers?

Alreck, P. L., & Settle, R. B. (1985). *The survey research handbook.* Homewood, IL: R. D. Irwin.
All of Chapter 2 pertains to project planning.

Fink, A. (1995). *The survey handbook.* Thousand Oaks: Sage Publications.
Provides information on why the survey is being conducted (pp. 81-82).

Chapter 2

Assess the Available Resources

Based on the considerations in Chapter 1, the survey developer should then focus attention on the amount of time and money needed to satisfy the objectives fully and completely. Before a researcher plunges into conducting a survey, an assessment of the resources (money, time, and availability of experts) should be made. If these resources are not available, then adjustments must be made; otherwise initial efforts may go for naught. Some resources may be difficult to assess, and in our experience our estimates are usually way too low. More people usually need to be surveyed than originally estimated because of low return rates. Data gathering often requires more time than anticipated. Data analysis and report writing also may take much longer.

Whatever task you delegate to others, either free or for pay, usually takes longer than if you were to do the task yourself. Why? No one cares as much about your survey as you do. This survey is your baby, and you are very proud of it. You want to see it mature, graduate into a report, and be useful to the intended stakeholders. Others are convinced that their babies are cuter (and smarter) than yours. You feel that way about their babies, right? Human nature at its best–or worst–depending upon your point of view. Had enough with this analogy?

Some answers to the resource availability questions will depend on decisions discussed in later chapters. For example, the method of collecting data (Chapter 5) will have financial and time implications. Mailed surveys cost less than telephone surveys. But telephone surveys allow for clarification and follow-up questions. As often happens, the least expensive method is not always the preferred choice.

As much as possible, one needs to plan for the entire survey process-from meeting with stakeholders, to analyzing the data, to preparing the report. All these endeavors have associated with them either time, money, or both time and money considerations. To arrive at this estimate, the following questions must be answered:

Question 4. What assistance do I need in surveying people?

Question 5. What types of analyses are required?

Question 6. Are computer programs available?

Question 4. What assistance do I need in surveying people?

Better to ask twice than to lose your way once. **Danish Proverb**

As discussed above, try to reduce the reliance upon other people. Invariably, though, you will need to obtain the assistance of people to do routine activities (e.g., copying, collating, mailing, data entry) or to guide you in technical or advanced survey issues (such as item format or procedures for follow-up).

Since the psychologist is doing a needs assessment to decide his own future employment, he should need little assistance. He will be combining subjectively the data he collects. Furthermore, one needs clinical training to make adequate diagnoses and therefore using untrained assistance is out of the question. He may need some assistance in getting to the clients, but would likely do all the surveying himself.

The administrative survey of superintendents will require the cooperation of the state superintendents' organization. The stakeholder's request to add an academic outcome item may require outside assistance, but probably can be done by the researcher. Depending upon skill level, time availability, and number of superintendents, assistance may be needed in the printing and distribution of the surveys.

The curriculum evaluator may need help in administering the survey in some schools. If the Old Curriculum was carried out in, say, 20 different schools, then it would be difficult for one person to travel to each of those 20 schools. A better procedure for her would be to hire data collectors, or to mail the survey. She is also going to need to get access to each school, so assistance will be needed. These issues are summarized in Exhibit 5.

Question 5. What types of analyses are required?

There are two kinds of statistics, the kind you look up and the kind you make up.   **Rex Stout**

It wasn't until late in life that I discovered how easy it is to say, "I don't know."   **W. Somerset Maugham**

The psychologist will be doing subjective analyses of client needs. The psychologist must relate those needs to his skills, his interests, and perceived amount of money that can be made. Since the only stakeholder in this example is the psychologist, he will be the one analyzing the data and determining if there is a critical mass of clients.

The administrator will need to record the percent agreement with each item on the school uniform survey. This might be completed by hand. The additional request to report the data broken down by rural-urban may make data entry and computer analysis more cost-effective.

Since the curriculum evaluator wants to assess the value of the New Curriculum, and she is interested in inferring to future years, she will need to rely on statistical analysis, and will undoubtedly use computer processing. The answers to the resource availability questions are summarized in Exhibit 5.

Exhibit 5

Summary of Answers to the "Resource Availability" Questions

Question 4. What assistance do I need in surveying people?
    Psychologist-How to get to clients.
    Administration-Cooperation of state organization.
    Curriculum-Help in administering surveys and access to all schools.

Question 5. What types of analyses are required?
    Psychologist-None.
    Administration-Proportions, by hand or computer.
    Curriculum-Statistical inference, computer processing needed (may need statistical consultant).

Question 6. Are computer programs available?
    Psychologist-Not relevant question.
    Administration-Yes, basic proportions.
    Curriculum-Yes, but probably rely on statistical consultant.

Question 6. Are computer programs available?

The world is rapidly wiring itself into one huge computer complex, and in this environment the most valuable future commodity promises to be hard, fresh data.   **Timothy Harris**

The psychologist does not need a computer program, as he will be making decisions strictly on his own judgment. There is no baseline for him to compare to. And if his decision is wrong, then he is the only one to suffer.

The school uniform study requires only basic percentages for the total group, and also for the rural and urban superintendents. As indicated above, the statistics could be computed by hand, or by computer program (such as PROC FREQ in SAS).

The curriculum evaluation relies on statistical hypothesis testing, so it would be recommended to use a computer statistical package (such as PROC TTEST in

SAS). The question to be answered in the curriculum evaluation is, "Are the differences between the two groups of teachers using the two curricula greater than would be expected through random fluctuations?" Unless statistical and computer skills have been acquired, one would likely want to consult with one who has those skills.

Summary of Resource Availability

To make the estimate as realistic as possible, expert advice should be sought from a research bureau, a statistical or computer center, or an individual who has completed a survey. These estimates should then be compared with the actual amount of time and money available. It is at this point that the procedures may need to be revised to be brought in line with the realistic resource limitations.

Additional Reading

Question 4. What assistance do I need in surveying people?

Alreck, P. L., & Settle, R. B. (1985). *The survey research handbook.* Homewood, IL: R. D. Irwin.
   Chapter 2 contains a discussion on "resource availability and costs."

Frey, J. H., & Oishi, S. M. (1995). *How to conduct interviews by telephone and in person.* Thousand Oaks, CA: Sage Publications.
   Good discussion of availability of resources (pp. 18-20).

Chapter 3

Define the Population

Based on the revised procedures of the survey (the result of Steps 1 and 2), one should delineate the characteristics of the population under investigation by considering such variables as age, gender, race, socioeconomic status, religion, occupation, and education. When delineating the population, one must also decide the geographic boundaries the researcher will work within. These boundaries must be congruent with the stated objectives.

There will be conditions for participation in every survey. Since it is not ethical to throw data away, one should identify these conditions for participation before the survey is administered and send the survey only to those meeting all the conditions. If you cannot identify those that meet the conditions before soliciting responses, then items on the survey should direct the respondent to stop responding if the respondent does not meet any one of the conditions for participation, as illustrated in Exhibit 6.

Exhibit 6. Procedures for Determining if Respondent Meets Conditions of Participation

Psychologist's in-person interview: "Is there a mental health rider in your company's insurance?" [If no then:] "Can you afford to pay for mental health services on your own?" [If no then stop the interview.]

Administrator's mailed survey: "If you have not thought about the effects of school uniforms until just now, mark 'NO' for this question and go to the last page. [Last page instructions: "You have finished the survey. Please return all of the survey, even if you have not answered some of the questions."]

Evaluation phone survey: "Did you faithfully follow the sixth-grade curriculum for at least 80% of the time?" [If answer is "YES" continue. If answer is "NO" ask "Why not?"]

Some conditions for participation that are sometimes not considered are whether the respondent has knowledge or an opinion on the topic, or whether they even understand the question. If they are not old enough to vote, for instance, then you would not be interested in for whom they would vote. Also, if they have not voted in the last 10 elections, you probably are not interested in for whom they would vote.

In almost every case, the accessible population is in some ways different from the population to which you want to generalize. Most statistics texts discuss taking a random sample from the population to which you want to generalize. Given that all interesting populations exist only in the future, we can never sample from the population to which we want to generalize. The concern is the extent to which you anticipate the accessible population being different from the population to which you want to generalize. Do you expect younger people to join the population next year? Might the new population members be more liberal? If so, then survey information should be weighted by those anticipated changes (a notion beyond the scope of this text).

The primary way that every accessible population is different from the population to which you want to generalize is that of volunteering. Every research study has volunteers. Research participants have the right to withdraw from a research study any time. If they stay, they have volunteered to stay! This becomes particularly apparent when some participants volunteer to leave, clearly implying that the others have volunteered to stay.

With respect to surveys, nonvolunteers are people who do not return mailed surveys, those who hang up on the telephone interviewer (or do not have a phone), those who do not make their appointment for an interview, and those who fail to answer all of the survey information. The concern is how these nonvolunteers are different from the volunteers, with respect to the issues being investigated. Since you do not have data from the nonvolunteers, it is often difficult to address this concern. Alternative data collection procedures (as in comparing demographic data, if they are available) is one way to decide if there are any differences between volunteers and nonvolunteers.

Population Questions to Answer

Defining the population can be conceptualized by answering the following questions:

Question 7. What is the population to which I am interested in generalizing?

Question 8. What are the characteristics of the population to which I am interested in generalizing?

Question 9. How does the accessible population differ from the population to which I want to generalize?

Question 10. How has volunteering affected my results?

Question 7. What is the population to which I am interested in generalizing?

A widely broadcast questionnaire is usually unavailable for anything more than obtaining of raw material of the statistician. . . . It may furnish confirmation of hypotheses, but it is very rare that it brings to light facts of structure and function not already within the knowledge of the investigator, or at least definitely suspected . . . to exist.
Sidney and Beatrice Webb

The psychologist is interested in generalizing to his clients (in that geographic area) in the immediate future. He knows that there will be some counseling issues that he is either not prepared to remediate, or does not care to remediate. He needs to decide if there are a sufficient number of clients that want his services, at least in the immediate future.

The stakeholders in the administrative survey of school uniforms are not interested in all current superintendents. The population of interest is actually next year's superintendents, and superintendents in the following years. Some turnover is to be expected, but there is no way to survey the attitudes of superintendents who are not now serving as a superintendent, but will be in one or two years. Thus, even if the entire current population can be surveyed, the entire population to which you want to generalize to cannot be surveyed. This is true in all research, not just survey research.

The curriculum evaluator's population is all sixth-grade teachers in that district in future years. As in the above example, all of next year's sixth-grade teachers cannot be surveyed. It is probably reasonable to assume that the new sixth-grade teachers will not be any different (with respect to evaluation of the New Curriculum) than those who are no longer sixth-grade teachers.

Question 8. What are the characteristics of the population to which I am interested in generalizing?

Up in the hills a census taker stops at a house and asks the woman how many people live there. "Well, let's see. There's me and Pa. There's Billy Bob, Sissy, the twins, Ricky and Micky, and there's Tommy and . . ."
"Hold on," interrupts the census taker. "I don't need names-just numbers."
"We don't use numbers," says the woman. "We ain't run out of names yet." **Source Unknown**

The psychologist is concerned about the immediate geographic area. He is also interested in people who are willing to discuss problems. Finally, and of most importance, the people must have some means for paying for their services.

The school uniform survey would be sent to all superintendents in the state. Though opinions of retiring superintendents or superintendents who have just moved from another state might be less important, the desire of the superintendent board to include all superintendents would supersede omitting any category of superintendents.

The curriculum evaluator would want to make sure that the teachers had used either the New Curriculum or the Old Curriculum for a minimum amount of time. Just because someone is trained in a method and told to use that method does not mean that that method will be used. And if the method has not been used, then the individual probably does not have a valid opinion of that method, and you probably should not be interested in that person's opinion. In Exhibit 6 we used the criterion of implementation of at least 80% of the time. There is nothing sacred about that figure, but 80% reflects the realization that no one can carry out something 100% of the time (especially the first year). We did not choose a lower figure because if you stray from implementation often, you cannot validly comment on the utility of that implementation. A summary of these answers and also answers to the remaining questions regarding defining the population appear in Exhibit 7.

Exhibit 7

Summary of Answers to the "Population" Questions

Question 7. What is the population to which I am interested in generalizing?
 Psychologist-All clients in the future.
 Administration-Superintendents in that state in the future.
 Curriculum-All teachers in sixth grade in future years.

Question 8. What are the characteristics of the population to which I am interested in generalizing?
 Psychologist-Immediate community so clients can get to office. Ability to pay or have insurance.
 Administrator-All current superintendents in state.
 Curriculum evaluator-Need to verify that teacher used the right curriculum a minimum percentage of the time.

Question 9. How does the accessible population differ from the population to which I want to generalize?
 Psychologist-Cannot interview all potential clients, but that is not a problem if get a sufficient number.
 Administrator-Unlikely that there are subtle year-to-year changes.
 Curriculum evaluator-Teachers who used New Curriculum likely volunteered, and may be more progressive and be in schools where a progressive behavior is

encouraged. Also, likely to be less enthralled with the Old Curriculum.

Question 10. How has volunteering affected my results?

Psychologist-Probably not in any systematic way.

Administrator-If superintendent knows the desire of the superintendents' state board, then more likely may respond if have opinion opposite to the board.

Curriculum evaluator-If teacher perceives that decision has been made already, or that teacher's opinions will not be considered, then may not respond to the survey (or may not respond honestly).

Question 9. How does the accessible population differ from the population to which I want to generalize?

USA Today has come out with a new survey-apparently, three out of every four people make up 75% of the population.   **David Letterman**

For the psychologist this does not seem to be a crucial question. If he can identify a substantial clientele from those he interviews, that should suffice. There may be a problem if all of the people in the geographic area who had his "special problem" went to be interviewed, leaving no others in the area with the same problem. In this scenario, he has exhausted the (immediate) supply of his "special problem."

In the school uniform study, a list of all current superintendents would be obtained. And there would be little reason to expect major differences in superintendents in the next few years. Some subsets of the superintendent group may not like the superintendents' state board, and may ignore requests to comply with surveys blessed by the state board. Working closely with the stakeholders should alert you to those kinds of problems.

The curriculum evaluation has the potential for a flaw, not in the survey itself but in the design of the study. If only a few teachers carry out the New Curriculum, who would they be? Randomly selected teachers? Not likely. These teachers likely would be in schools whose principals support innovation. And the teachers themselves likely would be ones who are progressive, and are particularly unhappy with the Old Curriculum. Teachers newer to the profession would more likely try the New Curriculum. And at the end of one year of use, they would be inclined to like it because of the time and energy invested in the New Curriculum.

Question 10. How has volunteering affected my results?

A survey of university professors found that 94% thought they were better at their jobs than their average colleague.   **T. Gilovich**

Volunteers for the psychologist's survey, unless they knew of his particular area of expertise, probably have not affected the results of the survey. Most applications in the social sciences can only serve volunteers anyway. So volunteering is an accepted condition of participation in many studies in the social sciences.

If a superintendent had an opinion regarding school uniforms that is different from those on the superintendent's state board, then that superintendent may choose not to respond to the survey. On the other hand, if that superintendent is particularly upset about the issue, a response may be returned immediately and with many comments in the margins.

The curriculum evaluation survey may also be influenced by perceptions of the respondent as they are perceived to be related to those of the person phoning or those in charge of making the decisions on whether to adopt the New Curriculum district-wide. Such perceptions often have a large influence on the results of research and have come to be called "demand characteristics" (Rosnow & Rosenthal, 1997).

Summary of Population Issues

The researcher should attempt to locate an adequate, up-to-date listing of the specified population. This is essential to the drawing of an appropriate sample. Lists such as telephone directories and organizational memberships can sometimes be obtained through federal, state, or local channels. It is very important that these lists represent the population to be investigated. It is crucial that the list be carefully scrutinized for its potential biases and representativeness before it is used. Finally, one should always realize that there will be some nonvolunteers. If there are nonvolunteers, then some effort should be made to detect how they are different from those who voluntarily provided the survey data.

Additional Reading

Question 9. How does the accessible population differ from the population to which I want to generalize?

Berdie, D. R., Anderson, J. F., & Niebuhr, M. A. (1986). *Questionnaires: Design and use.* (2nd ed.). Metuchen, NJ: The Scarecrow Press, Inc.
    In the discussion of nonrespondents, a research study is summarized on why late respondents do not provide a suitable basis for understanding nonrespondents (p. 100).

Goudy, W. J. (1977). *Nonresponse effect: Studies of the failure of potential respondent to reply to survey instruments.* Monticello, IL: Council of Planning Librarians.

Question 10. How has volunteering affected my results?

Fowler, F. J. (1995). *Improving survey questions: Design and evaluation.* Thousand Oaks, CA: Sage Publications.

Discusses bias due to nonresponse. Provides suggestions on how to reduce nonresponse.

Rossi, P. H., Wright, J. D., & Anderson, A. B. (1983). *Handbook of survey research.* New York: Academic Press.

An entire chapter is devoted to procedures for analyzing missing data.

Chapter 4

Review the Pertinent Literature

When reviewing the literature, one quite often can become frustrated in trying to decide how to best allocate available time. A search of the literature often uncovers many more references that appear to be appropriate than actually are. Some references may be only partially relevant. A well thought-out plan can save not only valuable time, but produce a better survey. Such a plan can help the researcher in identifying the most appropriate sources beforehand.

In this age of information, there are many references that can be of assistance. Also, various computerized search procedures are available. Finally, the World Wide Web can lead to sources that can be followed up on a more personal basis. Indeed, much more information exists than you probably have time or inclination to digest. Nevertheless, a plan should be developed so that you can build on the work previously accomplished. Too often, developers of surveys just "throw together some items," without avoiding the pitfalls that others have paved over. You are most likely to produce useful results if you use (or modify) an existing survey.

The literature search may yield no relevant information related to your survey. On the other hand, the search may provide enough evidence to make your survey unnecessary. Most literature searches end somewhere between these two extremes, yielding (a) surveys that can be adapted, (b) items that can be included, or (c) an approach to obtaining information that would be applicable for your problem.

Questions about Review of Pertinent Literature

Three major questions must be answered to conduct a fruitful literature search. The answers to these questions provide a plan for conducting the literature search so that you can optimize your time:

Question 11. Where can I look for information?

Question 12. What are the key terms for my literature search?

Question 13. What are the best sources of information?

Places to Look for Information

There are three major places to look for information. First, one can look in central sources. Central sources are databases that contain thousands of references and brief abstracts to journal articles, books, dissertations, and other manuscripts. Educational Resource Information Center (ERIC), Psychological Abstracts, Sociological Abstracts, and Dissertation Abstracts International are examples of the many central sources valuable to the helping professions.

Books and journals are the second category. Most libraries have an automated search capacity for books. A good focused source is PsychBOOKS, which contains a complete bibliographical citation, table of contents, and short statement about book content for single-author books.

Review journals contain summaries of the relevant research on selected topics. The Annual Review of Psychology, Review of Educational Research, and Social Service Review are but three examples of review journals.

The third way of obtaining information is directly from others in the field. This can be accomplished by attending conferences, by phone, or by writing. How would you discover with whom to talk? Your library searches discussed above or conference attendance would identify these persons. A recent trend is for some of these experts to make themselves available on the Internet. Indeed, searching the World Wide Web and following up on identified resources can often be fruitful.

Electronic Sources

The Internet has become a useful source of information. Many researchers have discovered that a general search will result in too many possible sources. Fortunately most search engines allow for Boolean logic, which will result in obtaining a smaller list of possible sources that are more likely to be relevant to your needs. Most engines use AND, OR, NOT, and NEAR, and also parentheses. The HELP section of the search engine you are using should tell you what Boolean options are available. Appendix A contains more detailed information on various search engines, tutorials on using search engines, and techniques to use in constraining searches. As in any search effort, you need to know what you want before you begin your search.

Question 11. Where can I look for information?

Knowledge is of two kinds: we know a subject ourselves, or we know where we can find information upon it.   **Samuel Johnson**

The psychologist should know how to classify the various mental health problems, but he might want to brush up on interviewing techniques by reading the Interviewer's Manual (Survey Research Center, 1976). If he could find a published survey conducted in the same community then he would not have to conduct his own needs assessment. A national survey would also be of value if he felt that his community was not that different from the rest of the nation in terms of mental health problems.

The ERIC central source would be the initial place for the administrator to go because her issue is an educational one. Regional and national conferences might produce some relevant references that did not find their way into ERIC. Finally, since school uniforms was a "hot topic" in the late 1990s, a search of the World Wide Web would likely produce some references. One should remember, though, that most information on the web is not refereed and therefore may contain inaccuracies. A search of the web in March of 1998 yielded 1,547,302 hits for the term "school uniform."

ERIC may also be a valuable resource for information on the utility of the two curricula. The companies that sell the curricula also can probably share evaluation information (information that needs to be digested with several grains of salt). Of particular value would be other schools that have evaluated either of the curricula. Some may have even compared the two. Another benefit from contacting other schools would be to learn of any incidental outcomes of the curricula. Of final value would be to learn of instruments used successfully. Why invent any more wheels than are necessary? If none of these sources produce any information of value, then the curriculum evaluator will have to develop her own survey.

Question 12. What are the key terms for my literature search?

In science, each new point of view calls forth a revolution in nomenclature.   **Friedrich Engles**

The availability of computerized searches can simplify the literature search. Knowing how to do a search is critical, as one can get lost, flooded with references, or obtain no references at all. The key to a literature search is planning the search by selecting the right key terms and right Boolean connectors (see Wilkinson & McNeil, 1996 for detail on both topics).

In our experience, the same key terms are not equally effective in two different central sources. Additionally, it may take several attempts before the "right" key terms are found. A computerized search should be an interactive search-reading references found on the first search to identify other key terms to use on subsequent searches.

When searching through test collections or conference proceedings, use the table of contents and index. Many of us fail to rely on these wonderful organizers. Those who plunge right in reference collections without relying on the table of contents or the index waste valuable time attending to irrelevant material.

The same comment can be made about World Wide Web searches. Because of the multitude of sites that are usually identified with a World Wide Web search, one should learn how to quickly read the abstract to make the decision about whether to access that site. Each site that is accessed takes time to make the connection and time to make the decision about whether it is a useful site.

If the psychologist cannot find an already completed survey, then he should begin his interviewing. His survey has implications for him and him alone. He does not have time to conduct an extensive review of literature as he must decide quickly if there are enough potential clients for him to open his business.

Since the administrator is interested in school uniforms and their impact on academic performance, these would be the two key terms that should be searched in ERIC. One might first search on "school uniforms OR dress codes" to see how many references there are to one or the other of these two key terms. If only 10 references are found, then she might want to read at least the abstract of those 10. But if many references are found, then she should consider adding "AND achievement." The AND connector limits the inclusion for those references that discuss either "school uniforms" or "dress codes" as well as "achievement."

If the ERIC search produces little information, she has another route available. ERIC has a service called "ask ERIC" that provides reference librarians to look up your particular topic. They are paid by the Federal government, are highly qualified, and have many resources available to them.

The curriculum evaluator's key terms would be "Old Curriculum OR New Curriculum AND evaluation." Unfortunately, the two curricula would likely not be in the Thesaurus of Key Terms. The "ask ERIC" service can assist her. The search may have to start with conference programs for curriculum, program evaluation, or educational research. Each of these conferences has divisions, sections, or special interest groups that focus on evaluation of particular curricula. Informal networks of school district evaluators might identify other resources for the curriculum evaluator.

Question 13. What are the best sources of information?

The rules of the game: learn everything, read everything, inquire into everything. . . . When two texts, or two assertions, or perhaps two ideas, are in contradiction, be ready to reconcile them rather than cancel one by the other; regard them as two different facets, or two successive stages, of the same reality, a reality convincingly human just because it is complex.

Marguerite Yourcenar

It is a given that there are many resources for almost any endeavor, and that is also true for survey research. Unfortunately, many people act as if anyone can develop a survey, and that the development does not need any technical assistance. Survey development is partly art, but it is mostly science. There are many references available to help in each step in survey research. Since this text is intended to be an overview of the process, each survey developer should rely on other resources to help in any step of the survey that seems too problematic.

Entire books exist for each step that we have identified, and in some cases for some specific questions. We have identified at the end of each chapter what we consider good resources for each specific question.

The psychologist could best benefit from a reference on interviewing. He wants to obtain information from as few people as possible, since each interview will take time and delay him from starting his business. He must gain rapport, obtain their trust, and make sure that their responses are the correct responses. That is, the psychologist must be assured that each person answered the questions in the way that was right for them.

The administrator surveying attitudes toward school uniforms should refer to a resource that can guide her in survey development. In reading such a resource, she will discover that item format and item order are particularly important in mailed surveys (more on mailed surveys in Chapter 5). The cover letter also will be particularly crucial for this survey, as the topic of school uniforms is controversial.

The curriculum evaluator should search for existing instruments. A source such as the Educational Testing Service collection may provide some possibilities. Also, contacting other school evaluators at the local or state level may produce some existing surveys or at least some good ideas. Item construction is also an important consideration as respondents may have reasons for not answering 100% truthfully.

Teachers may be so upset with the Old Curriculum that they would prefer any other curriculum, despite existing data demonstrating that it benefited the students. Or, teachers may not like the New Curriculum just because they think the administration wants them to prefer the New Curriculum.

Teachers may also report that they prefer the New Curriculum just because they invested time in understanding the New Curriculum. (I've spent so much money for this new outfit that I'd better like it.) This phenomenon is called "cognitive dissonance."

Summary of Review of the Pertinent Literature

By now the novice survey developer should realize that you cannot just "throw some items together." As we have suggested, there is some art in the process, but there is a large base of science and recommended procedures that have worked in other surveys.

Additional Reading

Question 11. Where can I look for information?

Conoley, J. C., & Impara, J. C. (Eds.). (1995). *The twelfth mental*

measurements yearbook. Lincoln, NE: The University of Nebraska Press.
   Provides a bibliography on 418 tests, and 803 critical reviews.

   Goldman, B. A., & Osbourne, W. (1985). *Unpublished mental measurements*
(Vol 4). New York: Human Sciences Press, Inc.
   Provides reviews on various topical areas. Some critiques focus on specific
tests, while others cover broad areas.

   Keyser, D. J., & Sweetland, R. C. (Eds.). (1986). *Tests: A comprehensive
reference for assessment in psychology, education, and business.* Kansas City,
MO: Test Corporation of America.
   Format similar to *Mental measurements yearbooks*, containing information
on over 3,500 tests.

   Murphy, L. L., Conoley, J. C., & Impara, J. C. (1994). *Tests in print IV.*
Lincoln, NE: The University of Nebraska Press.
   A good resource for tests that have already had some psychometric work
completed.

   Robinson, J. P., Shaver, P. R., & Wrightsman, L. S. (1991). *Measures of
personality and social psychological attitudes.* New York: Academic Press.
   Provides evaluations of the measures, as well as sample items in some
cases.

Question 12. What are the key terms for my literature search?

   Wilkinson, W. K., & McNeil, K. (1996). *Research methods for the helping
professions.* Pacific Grove, CA: Brooks/Cole.
   Chapter 2 covers how to identify key terms in your research, and how to use
those in searching electronic databases.

Question 13. What are the best sources of information?

   Fink, A. (1995). *The survey handbook.* Thousand Oaks, CA: Sage.
   Discusses advantages of various sources of information.

   Wilkinson, W. K., & McNeil, K. (1996). *Research methods for the helping
professions.* Pacific Grove, CA: Brooks/Cole.
   Chapter 2 provides electronic sources, and Chapter 4 provides text sources.

Chapter 5

Determine the Data Collection Techniques

This chapter first discusses the various procedures that can be used to administer the survey. There are four basic ways to collect survey information: (1) mail, (2) direct administration, (3) telephone, and (4) interview. Next, the value of using an existing survey is discussed. The chapter concludes with a discussion of who should administer the survey.

Mailed Surveys

One of the most frequently used surveys is the mailed survey. It is the most widely used technique in the social sciences. In part, its popularity may be due to the mistaken belief that it can be easily constructed. Unfortunately, many surveys of this type have been hastily thrown together, resulting in ambiguous questions that produce negative attitudes in the respondents. These attitudes then tend to lead to one of two outcomes: (1) the responses are biased and, therefore, are not representative, or (2) the survey is thrown away by many. In either case, conclusions would be incorrect. An advantage to this type of survey is that a large sample can be reached in an economical manner.

The developer of a well-constructed mailed survey must allow for many factors. It should be accompanied by a brief, nontechnical cover letter clearly explaining its purpose and relevance. If this letter can be written on official stationary and signed or endorsed by a well-known figure relevant to the topic, then the return rate will be increased.

The developer of the survey should be concerned about aspects such as length, pertinence, clarity, and types of responses. Evidence suggests that long surveys are less likely to be returned-responding time for a survey should not exceed 20 minutes. This time estimate should be adjusted depending on the audience, the purpose, and how crucial it is to obtain the results. Since the survey may give the appearance of requiring more response time than it actually takes, the survey developer may choose to include in the cover letter information concerning the expected amount of time needed to complete the survey.

One way to control for the length is to make sure everything asked is pertinent to the objectives underlying the study. This is not only a crucial aspect-it is a difficult aspect. Following is a procedure that may be helpful in developing clear and pertinent objectives.

1. First, reexamine your objectives and purpose so that you will be better prepared to evaluate any items in terms of their relevance.

2. To generate questions, an open-ended survey may be administered to a small sample of the population of interest, or to a small group of experts. Here the questions are presented in a way that resembles an essay test format. These lengthy responses are then analyzed in terms of their relevance to the objectives. They are then categorized for transforming them into what are sometimes called closed-ended questions, questions that are more like a multiple choice item. This format is considered more desirable for a survey as it is easier for the respondent to answer, and it is easier for the researcher to tabulate and analyze the data.

3. Once the closed-ended questions are developed, they should be piloted with another small sample from the population of interest. This sample should be timed so that an estimate of the amount of time required to respond to the survey is known. The respondents then should be interviewed to detect if there were any (a) ambiguous questions, (b) problems in understanding the questions, (c) threatening or embarrassing questions, or (d) suggestions for revision.

4. Based on the above information, revisions in the survey should be made. Particular attention should be given to questions interpreted as either threatening or embarrassing. If possible, these questions should be omitted. If they are determined to be crucial to the study, they should be placed as close to the end of the survey as possible. The promise of anonymity may reduce some negative feelings associated with responding to such questions.

There are two major disadvantages to using mailed surveys. The first is that the return rate is generally quite low. Heberlein and Baumgartner (1978) report a synthesis of the literature on nonrespondents and suggest that the average return rate for the first mailing is 48%. One wonders about the validity of generalizing from this (likely biased) set of responses to the entire population. One way of improving the return rate is by sending follow-up letters, cards, and surveys. The follow-up mailing should restate the purpose of the survey in clear and nontechnical terms. It may state a reasonable deadline for the return and may again offer to share the survey findings. Floyd and Fowler (1993) report that the first follow-up will result in 63% return rate, the second in 83% return rate, and the third in 96% return rate. One might wonder, though, if these later returns have been filled out as validly as those that were first returned. Obviously there is increased cost with each follow-up.

The second limitation to mailed surveys is more ominous. There is generally no way for the researcher to check the accuracy of the responses. Because of these two limitations, we think if it is possible, other procedures for collecting the survey information should be used. If other procedures have been ruled out, it is essential that either at least 80% return rate be achieved or characteristics of those who have not responded be obtained. Gathering information about the people who did not respond enables the researcher to place limitations on generalizations that will make the interpretations more accurate.

Directly Administered Surveys

It may be the case that the survey can be administered directly. Such a situation would be administering a survey to students in a classroom, or at a meeting of the group to which the results are to be generalized.

For purposes of construction and format, the procedures for developing such surveys are identical to those suggested for mailed surveys. The major difference between the two is that poor return rate is generally not a problem with directly administered surveys. When possible and appropriate, directly administered surveys should be preferred to mailed surveys.

Telephone Surveys

Telephone surveys are popular because information can be quickly obtained and because such surveys are inexpensive to conduct. They are only appropriate when simple and superficial information is needed and only a few questions have to be asked.

Again, check your objectives to decide if a few simple questions are sufficient to gather the information. If these questions do not require in-depth responses, then a telephone survey may be appropriate. However, it should be recognized that people tend to be uncooperative in providing information over the phone and this may be a major limitation for your survey.

Interview Surveys

Interview surveys are those that are conducted in person, with one respondent at a time. Such interviews require social skills and quick-thinking by the interviewers. Procedures for interviewing can be divided into three broad categories: 1) structured, (2) partially structured, and (3) unstructured.

The structured interview is constructed using the same considerations as mailed and directly administered surveys. The structured interview consists of an interviewer reading the questions, possible answers, and recording the answers. This type of interview is most appropriate when one is not interested in attitudes or personal feelings. The structured interview has the advantage that the interviewer can gain additional information, such as how the respondent interpreted the question and what was meant by the responses (using follow-up questions).

The partially structured interview is similar to the structured interview in that both have a core of objectives around which the questions are built. The difference is that the interviewer in the partially structured interview is interested in the reasons behind the responses and will try to explore those reasons in depth. This procedure requires extensive training to achieve a high degree of skill by the interviewer.

The effectiveness of the unstructured interview in gathering information is totally dependent on the skill and training of the interviewer. There is no basic core of questions; the procedure is primarily useful when the purpose is to obtain highly personal information, such as in surveys on sexual behavior.

Only the structured interview will be discussed in detail since an integral part of the other two procedures is dealing with how to train an interviewer, which deviates from the purpose of this text. Further information on the other techniques is contained in the references at the end of the chapter.

When using an interview procedure, as in other survey procedures, it is extremely important that the questions be consistent with the objectives. One approach to accomplishing this is to take the general objectives and rewrite then into more detailed objectives. Once specificity is achieved, these objectives can be reworded and refined to become the core questions of the interview. One should also follow the same procedure as discussed for mailed surveys: (1) identify pertinent questions, (2) pilot these questions, and (3) then rewrite and redefine them based on the information received from the pilot survey.

The major advantage of the interview over the other survey procedures is that the interviewer can obtain insight into why the respondent answered the way he or she did. For example, suppose the following question was asked, "Do you consider present-day education important?" Ten people may have answered "yes," but each may have a different reason for giving this response. The interview procedure has the unique advantage of allowing the investigation of these different motives. This important additional information allows the researcher to make more valid interpretations of the data, which can yield more meaningful solutions to the problem under study.

Some disadvantages of using interviews are that they require an inordinate amount of time and expense. When using the interview approach, it is crucial that the interviewer be well-trained. This training is both time-consuming and expensive, but it is essential if one is to have data that are reliable and valid. To ensure reliability of the data, the researcher must train the interviewers to ask the questions in as much the same way as possible to make sure that each question is presented to the respondents with the same frame of reference. Additional expense is incurred when the researcher feels that it is necessary to check the reliability of the data. This can be done by having more than one person interview the same respondent. The data are then compared to see if the responses are consistent.

The validity of the interview is generally controlled for by training the interviewers to be sensitive to their own biases, and by checking to make sure that the questions are not loaded with socially desirable or hidden biases. This simply means that the major estimates of validity for interviews tends to be content validity, not the strongest type of validity estimate.

It is appropriate to survey with an interview when one is interested in collecting data that tend to be of a sensitive nature, when dealing with children, and when there is no more appropriate procedure that is less expensive.

Comparison of the Four Survey Procedures

Exhibit 8 contains the rank order rating of the four survey procedures on several considerations. We have not ordered the considerations in any way, as different survey developers will be concerned about the considerations in very different ways. Furthermore, these ranks are estimates "on average." A particular survey may result in different estimates.

Exhibit 8

Considerations in the Selection of a Survey

Consideration	Directly	Phone	Mailed	Interview
Comparative cost	1	2.5	4	2.5
Facilities needed	yes	no	no	yes
Training needed	yes	yes	no	yes
Data collection time	1	2	3	4
Return rate	1.5	3	4	1.5
Group administer	yes	no	no	yes
Follow-up possible	no	yes	no	yes
Respondent bias	2.5	2.5	4	1
Researcher bias	2.5	2.5	1	4
Objectivity of responses	1.5	3	1.5	4

Note. Numbers in exhibit indicate rank order: 1= most positive; 4 = least positive. Adapted from Wilkinson and McNeil, 1996.

The two major considerations are time and cost. Both are reduced with directly administered surveys, therefore the rank of 1. The table also addresses a matter of great concern: return rate. Note that across the four procedures, return rates for directly administered surveys and interviews are the highest. On the other hand, return rate is a major concern when surveys are mailed.

Question 14. What survey procedure should I use?

I did that, says my memory. I could not have done that, says my pride,
and remains inexorable. Eventually the memory yields.   **Nietzsche**

The psychologist chooses to interview people in his office. He decides that a
phone survey would not be perceived as "professional" as an in-person interview.
A mailed survey would likely yield a very small return rate as respondents have
no reason to reply. Would you put that personal information in the mail? The
interview would allow him to ask some follow-up questions if there were any
concerns or misgivings. He would likely have to reimburse people for their
travel and time, but since all respondents would live in the same geographical
area as the psychologist, there would be little travel cost. Finally, the study can
easily be ended whenever the psychologist decides that he has enough
information to make his decision. Exhibit 9 summarizes the psychologist's
issues regarding survey procedure, and also those of the other researchers to be
discussed below.

Exhibit 9

Summary of Answers to the Question ,"What Survey Procedure Should I Use?"

Psychologist
    Follow-up questions would be valuable.
    Phone and mail yield low return rate.
    Travel to office by respondents not a problem if reimbursed.
    Therefore choice is interview in person in his office.

Administrator
    Travel to all schools in state prohibitive.
    Phone cost high and not interested in follow-up questions.
    Return rate high if mailed on board stationary and supported by board.
    Therefore choice is mailed survey.

Curriculum evaluator
    Phone survey allows for some follow-up.
    Little cost for local calls.
    Respondents know and trust caller.
    Note can be sent indicating when teachers can call her.
    Therefore choice is phone survey.

The administrator is charged with surveying all superintendents in the state. It would be prohibitive to travel to all the school districts to conduct interviews. It would also not be feasible to interview all the superintendents at the annual state convention, as they need to attend to the normal activities. Phone interviews would be costly, and she has visions of "phone tag" dancing in her head. Since she is not interested in any follow-up questions, she chooses to gather her survey information by mail. A disadvantage of mailed surveys is that return rate is often low. Since she has the support of the state superintendents' board, and they have agreed to let her use their stationary, she is expecting she will have a satisfactorily high return rate.

The curriculum evaluator decides to do a phone survey. While she could travel to all the schools, she does not see any advantage to a personal interview. All of the teachers to be interviewed know her and know that an evaluation of the two curricula is planned. She would like to have her survey be directly administered, but that would require all the teachers leaving their classrooms and converging on one site. She plans to send them a note with times that she can be reached by phone. Thus, the teachers can call her at a time convenient to them. This phone procedure will allow for some follow-up and can be conducted in a short period of time.

Question 15. Should I use an existing survey, or develop my own?

If none of the available instruments meets the needs of the researcher, the researcher is confronted with either having to alter the research question or to accomplish the difficult task of developing a measuring instrument. The usability of specially designed instruments may override the difficulty of establishing reliability and validity.

Wilkinson & McNeil

Besides deciding the method of collecting survey data, one needs to decide if an existing survey can be used, or if one needs to develop an entirely new survey. Unfortunately, most researchers believe that no adequate survey exists, and rush to develop their own. Throwing a survey together is a simple matter. Developing a reliable, valid, and usable survey is another matter. We recommend that effort be expended to learn if an adequate survey has already been developed. If one has, it may also be the case that there is some data from that survey that can be referred to in the current study—either as baseline or for comparison purposes. In addition, the prior use of the survey may have identified problems with some items. Current development effort (discussed in the next chapter), could focus on these problematic items.

The psychologist could very likely find the necessary survey questions. He is not the first psychologist investigating the possibility of starting a new business. Surely there is mention in the literature of other efforts. Furthermore, the psychologist's concerns would be similar to those of other helping professionals who are starting a new practice. Therefore there may be relevant surveys already used by other helping professionals, such as social workers, educational tutors, and nurses.

The administrator may find an existing survey, or at least adapt an existing survey to meet her needs and the peculiarities of the topic on which she is conducting her study. Due to the timeliness of the topic, and the particular concerns of the stakeholders, she will likely have to develop some survey items. She can, though, rely on the literature for item format, as well as all the mechanics (such as cover letter, incentives, and ethical issues). These concerns are summarized in Exhibit 10.

Exhibit 10

Summary of Answers to the Question, "Should I Use an Existing Survey, or Develop my Own?"

Psychologist
>   Little time and money to develop a good survey.
>   Models are available.
>   Therefore choice is to adapt an existing survey.

Administrator
>   Same topic unlikely surveyed.
>   State idiosyncrasies would likely require some item changes.
>   Stakeholder group requires certain information.
>   Therefore will likely adapt existing survey on same or similar topic.

Curriculum evaluator
>   No previous evaluation of New Curriculum has been reported.
>   Several surveys in the literature that compare teacher's perceptions of two different curricula are outdated.
>   Central administration and school board have specific questions they want answered.
>   Therefore choice is to develop completely new survey.

The curriculum evaluator would be encouraged to adopt an existing survey. Many school districts have evaluated the effectiveness of a curriculum. Some have included teacher's perceptions of the curriculum. Indeed, there is political advantage to adopting or adapting an existing survey, as those who think you may be 'stacking the cards against' one of the curricula have less room to challenge you.

Although the two curricula of concern may not have been evaluated, the curriculum evaluator could replace 'curriculum X' and 'curriculum Y' with 'New Curriculum' and 'Old Curriculum' and have a survey that is ready to use. Hopefully this survey had few or no technical problems when used previously.

While we encourage all survey researchers to search the literature for an existing survey to adopt or adapt, we realize that often the purpose of the survey, stakeholder's interests, or idiosyncrasies of the population or topic require a survey to be constructed. We conclude that this is the decision of the curriculum evaluator. The major considerations in survey development are discussed in the next chapter.

Question 16. Who should administer the survey?

[Any response] is only in part a function of . . . the questions. It is also a function of the social interaction of the interviewer's appearance, of the respondent's fear of similar strangers, such as bill collectors.
Donald T. Campbell

Our general recommendation is that the researcher should be involved in every step of the process. It is human nature to care more about an activity if you have ownership. Though you pay assistants, they often do not care, or do not know enough about the whole process to understand the implications of their actions. You, the survey researcher, understand the big picture, and are in a better position to make on-the-spot decisions that are in the best interest of the big picture.

Being involved in the administration of the survey will take time. Our experience is that it is time well spent. That way you can spot problems, and identify possible shortcuts. Participating also sends an encouraging word to your assistants.

The psychologist has little finances available to support the survey. The in-person interview requires disclosure of sensitive material and requires technical content knowledge by the interviewer. The psychologist could use the services of a secretary to make the appointments and greet the respondents. But he would have to conduct all of the survey interviews himself.

The administrator may have some financial support for the research from her university or from the state organization of superintendents. She could use this money for copying surveys, mailing, and data entry. She realizes, though, that each of these activities is crucial and can be conducted improperly. She therefore decides to hire one clerk and plans to be present whenever the clerk is working. She plans to be involved in each task.

The curriculum evaluator knows that the district wants the information and therefore she can justify her time and that of her secretary. Because of how crucial the information is and the fact that often respondents will not be anonymous, she decides to conduct the phone surveys herself. She feels that the trust developed over the years can be relied on to obtain useful information. A summary of these answers appears in Exhibit 11.

Exhibit 11

Summary of Answers to the Question, "Who Should Administer the Survey?"

Psychologist
    Little finances available to do survey.
    In-person survey requires content expertise.
    Secretary can help in making appointments and greeting respondents.
    Therefore the decision is that he will do all the interviews himself.

Administrator
    Some funds available from university and from the stakeholder association.
    Will hire clerk to copy cover letter and instrument, assemble mailing, and open returned mailed survey.
    Therefore she decides to be present and assist during all the clerk's activities.

Curriculum evaluator
    Since district wants information, secretary could be used to conduct phone survey.
    Sensitivity of information, and trust developed by evaluator leads to decision that evaluator will conduct the phone survey herself.

Additional Reading

Question 14. What survey procedure should I use?

Berdie, D. R., Anderson, J. F., & Niebuhr, M. A. (1986). *Questionnaires: Design and use* (2nd ed.). Metuchen, NJ: The Scarecrow Press, Inc.
    Chapter 3 posits the question, "Interview or mail?" Note that Chapter 5 contains a good overview of issues to consider when interacting with respondents (such as cover letters, printing of surveys, and incentives).

Bourque , L. B., & Fiedler, E. P. (1995). *How to conduct self-administered and mail surveys.* Thousand Oaks, CA: Sage Publications.
    A nice companion to the Fink and Oishi manual in that this one focuses on self-administered and mail surveys while the latter focuses on interviews.

Dillman, D. A. (1978). *Mail and telephone surveys: The total design method.* New York: Wiley

The classic in the field of developing your own mail or telephone survey.

Fink, A., & Oishi, S. M. (1995). *How to conduct interviews by telephone and in person.* Thousand Oaks, CA: Sage Publications.
Entire manual is devoted to actual conduct of the interview.

Fowler, F. J. (1995). *Improving survey questions: Design and evaluation.* Thousand Oaks, CA: Sage Publications.
Chapter 4 provides extensive list of advantages and disadvantages of each survey method.

Lavrakas, P. J. (1987). *Telephone survey methods: Sampling, selection, and supervision.* Newbury Park, CA: Sage.
Discusses questions in the context of telephone surveys.

Marshall, B. G. (1976). *Mail questionnaire research: A selected bibliography with selected annotations.* Monticello, IL: Council of Planning Librarians.

Rossi, P. H., Wright, J. D., & Anderson, A. B. (1983). *Handbook of survey research.* New York: Academic Press.
Chapter 10 covers mail and other self-administered surveys.

Question 15. Should I use an existing survey, or develop my own?

Rossi, P. H., Wright, J. D., & Anderson, A. B. (1983). *Handbook of survey research.* New York: Academic Press.
Chapters 6 and 7 cover such topics as question order and format, qualities of a good survey, and scaling techniques.

Sudman, S., & Bradburn, N. M. (1974). *Response effects in surveys: A review and synthesis.* Chicago: Aldine Publishing Company.
Provides a model of the interview, including task variables, role of the interviewer, and respondent role behavior. One chapter devoted to "effects of time and money factors on memory," and another on "the effect of respondent and interviewer characteristics on response to attitude questions."

Survey Research Center. (1976). *Interviewer's manual.* Ann Arbor, MI: Institute for Social Research, University of Michigan.
Provides many examples on all aspects of conducting interviews.

Question 16. Who should administer the survey?

Alwin, D. F. (1978). *Survey design and analysis: Current issues.* Beverly Hills, CA: Sage Publications.

Provides a good discussion of informed consent (pp. 59-80).

Frey, J. H., & Oishi, S. M. (1995). *How to conduct interviews by telephone and in person.* Thousand Oaks, CA:Sage Publications.
A lot of good information on interviewer selection, training, and supervision (pp. 109-146).

Chapter 6

Develop the Survey

This chapter discusses only a few of the many considerations one must ponder when developing a survey. As we have emphasized in the previous chapters, we strongly suggest adopting, or at least adapting an existing survey. Sometimes circumstances dictate that a survey be custom-developed to meet the basic questions that you want answered. Entire textbooks (some of which are annotated at the end of this chapter) discuss the development of surveys. Since this text is intended to get the survey researcher started, we focus only on the following four questions:

Question 17. What are the item format considerations?

Question 18. What are the psychometric considerations?

Question 19. What are the piloting considerations?

Question 20. What are the training considerations?

Item Format

There are four major ways that items can be presented to respondents. The item can be open-ended, which means that the respondent is asked a general question and might respond in many ways. The opposite to an open-ended item is a dichotomous-choice item; as when the respondent must choose between two alternatives. If socially desirable responses might occur, then the forced-choice item should be used. The fourth item format to be discussed is the scaled-choice format that allows more than two possible choices, usually 5 to 7.

Open-ended items allow respondents to give the amount of detail that they choose. Unfortunately, such detailed information is difficult to aggregate. The fact that the data are idiosyncratic means that two coders may not agree on the interpretation because there is no common reference point. The difficulty of summarization is further exacerbated because it is often difficult to fathom why respondents said what they did.

Dichotomous-choice items divide the universe of possible answers into two categories (usually true-false or yes-no). Since many different answers are forced to take on the same value, summary of the data is easy.

Forced-choice items demand that the respondent choose between two or more options. The best application of this item type is where the options can be viewed as equally positive options. The forced-choice item is particularly appropriate when respondents might try to give socially desirable responses. If the options are equally socially desirable, then the respondent must respond on some basis other than social desirability.

Scaled-choice items contain more than two points (such as Likert scales). Although respondents usually answer favorably, responses on such an item can be used to compare various samples or to compare different items within one survey. Appendix B provides many more detailed examples of various item formats.

Question 17. What are the item format considerations?

The extent to which the wording of questions affects the answers depends almost entirely on the degree to which the respondent's mental context is solidly structured. Where people have standards of judgment resulting in stable frames of reference, the same answer is likely to be obtained irrespective of the way questions are asked. . . . Where such standards of judgment are lacking, [people] are highly suggestible to the implications of phrases, statements, innuendoes or symbols of any kind that may serve as clues to help them make up their minds.

H. A. Cantril

The psychologist would be interested in using a combination of items (see Appendix C for his protocol). One dichotomous-choice item he might consider would be, "Have you ever had the problem of not being able to stop smoking?" Given that anxiety is a less concrete construct, he might want to put the response to that problem on a continuum, such as, "How often have you had the problem of anxiety?

1 = Never   2 = Seldom   3 = Sometimes   4 = Often

An open-ended question that the psychologist might use would be, "Since your hospitalization coverage doesn't cover any of the problems that we have discussed, how much would you be willing to pay to try to solve the problem?"

The school uniform study would best consist of any kind of item, except open-ended. Since responses are expected from each superintendent in the state, all those responses to an open-ended item would have to be coded. It is much easier to precode the responses by identifying expected responses before you send out the survey. These expected responses become the permissible responses. The intent of the school uniform survey is "to get the pulse" of all the superintendents in the state, not the detailed opinions of any one superintendent.

The researcher may want to include some forced-choice responses to prevent all responses from being socially desirable ones. The demographic items in Appendix D are both dichotomous-choice. The next five items in Appendix D are all scaled-choice. The last two items are forced-choice.

The curriculum evaluator will try to focus on dichotomous-choice and Likert-type items. Since two curricula are being compared, there is a built-in reference point (the Old Curriculum). Because the curriculum evaluator knows all the teachers, social desirability should not be a factor. The evaluator may want to include an item or two that is forced-choice to check on this. Because the curriculum survey is being done on the phone, the evaluator has the opportunity to ask open-ended questions and probe for clarity. Appendix E contains her script with the questions that she will be asking.

Psychometric Considerations

The three psychometric considerations (measurement considerations) are reliability, validity, and usability. Reliability means that the same response would be obtained on repeated attempts. Validity means that the survey item really does measure what you want it to measure. Reliability is a necessary condition for validity, but not a sufficient condition. That is, an item can be very reliable, but not measure what you want it to measure. If a survey item asks respondents what their shoe size is, we would expect to get nearly the same answer each time that the item was asked. The item is a reliable measure, and it is a valid measure of shoe size. But it is not a valid measure of many other traits, such as intelligence. Of most importance is the psychometric consideration of utility. Can the survey be used for the purpose intended? Usability subsumes the ideas of reliability and validity, and facilitates them.

Reliability. There are many different ways to calculate reliability, but most require more than one item of the construct. That is, there would need to be several items measuring the same construct. Reliability is greatly influenced by the nature of the persons responding to the survey and the context in which the survey is administered. Thus, reliability will be lower for younger respondents, lower for mailed surveys than phone surveys, and lower when the focus of the survey is not very salient to the respondents.

There are two ways of estimating reliability that are of interest to the survey researcher. The most common reliability index is that of the Cronbach Alpha. This measure can be used with dichotomous-choice and also scaled-choice items. It requires that the alternatives form a scale and that each respondent chooses only one alternative. The items scored together are assumed to be measuring the same construct-therefore a unidimensional scale. The Cronbach Alpha is essentially the average correlation among all the items that you identify to be measuring the same construct.

The second way of obtaining reliability is to ask the same question a second time (usually camouflaged). The percentage agreement of the responses to these two items is then reported. This method is preferred when you do not want to include many items about one construct.

Validity. Validity really has several aspects to it. First, there is content validity. Does the survey appear to the respondent that it looks like it measures what you want it to measure? This is a judgment call by content experts, presuming that they know how respondents will view the survey. Content validity does not provide a numerical number, just an indication of general agreement by experts in the content area.

A second measure of validity is construct validity. For this measure of validity, differences between groups expected to be different on the construct are checked out. For instance, if one has developed a survey on attitude toward gun control, there should be a difference on the survey between members of the National Rifle Association and those that are not.

Predictive validity is the last aspect of validity that we will discuss. This aspect focuses on individuals and assess the extent to which respondents with low scores would do differently in the future, as compared to those with high scores. This is an important notion, as surveys should not just identify what currently exists, but they should allow us to predict to future behavior. Unfortunately, few survey researchers follow up their respondents to see if survey responses predict subsequent behavior.

Usability. While reliability and validity are the true psychometric considerations, usability is the ultimate consideration. Usability entails all of the administration concerns, including administration, interpretation, reporting, and costs associated with each. For instance, if knowing how to administer a survey requires training (to be discussed at the end of this chapter), then either a trained test administrator must be hired, or the researcher must undergo training. Many surveys cannot be scored by hand, resulting in additional costs and potential delays. Reliability and validity often rely on standardized administration and scoring procedures, and therefore these standardized procedures must be followed if that survey is to be used. If the costs are judged to be too high, an alternate survey or survey method must be chosen.

Question 18. What are the psychometric considerations?

If a thing exists, it exists in some amount. If it exists in some amount, it can be measured.   **E. L. Thorndike**

I was gratified to be able to answer promptly, and I did. I said I didn't know.   **Mark Twain**

The psychologist can get an idea if his respondents are reliably answering the items by including also a slightly altered item. Indeed, one approach often used is to ask if a friend would also do that. Since the psychologist is wanting to get information about real behavior (in this hypothetical situation) such an approach might be quite valuable. Another validity check he might use is to watch for any nervous behavior when the respondents are answering his questions. The relaxed, businesslike atmosphere should provide usable information. In addition, the psychologist can follow up on responses to try to understand how he could make his services more attractive to clients (extended hours, location, etc.). All these psychometric considerations for each of the three vignettes are summarized in Exhibit 12.

Exhibit 12

Summary of Answers to the Psychometric Consideration Questions

---

Psychologist
   Reliability-ask same item twice
   Validity-hypothetical versus real behavior
   Validity-watch for behavior, such as squirming, deep swallows
   Usability-can get information from the responses as to how to make his service better

Administrator
   Reliability-multiple items measuring school uniform use
   Validity-compare rural and urban
   Validity-compare those who have had policy for 2 years to those who have never had policy
   Usability-determine through pilot if superintendents understand the items, have the information with which they can answer the item, and reasonable time frame in which to answer the items

Curriculum evaluator
   Reliability-during phone interview, ask same question again (pretending to not have written the first response down)
   Validity-correlate teachers' responses to improved student performance with standardized test scores
   Usability-pilot phone survey and learn ease with which curriculum evaluator can conduct phone survey

---

The school uniform survey has multiple measures of the same construct. Therefore, Cronbach Alpha can be computed for those scaled-choice items. Since the state board was interested in the responses of rural and urban superintendents, there should be some expected differences between their responses-an example of known-groups validity. Another example of known groups validity would be comparing the responses of those who have had a school uniform policy in effect for at least two years to those who have yet to set up such a policy. Usability of the survey should be decided through a pilot test with a small number of superintendents from a neighboring state by asking such questions as, "Do you feel that you understood each item," "Do you know enough about school uniforms to answer the items?" and "Were you able to complete the survey is a reasonable amount of time?"

The curriculum evaluator could also ask the same question twice during each phone survey, pretending to not have recorded the first response. To check on the validity of the teachers' responses to the effect of the curriculum on student performance, she could compare those responses with the actual student standardized test performance–data that she probably would want to discuss in her evaluation anyway. To improve the usability, she should conduct several practice interviews. Also, having the teachers call her makes the phone survey less intrusive for the teachers.

Piloting a Survey

The purpose of piloting a survey is to increase the reliability, validity, and usability of the survey. Any data gathering activity involves many steps, and the more steps that you can feel confident about, the smoother your data collection process will go. We will discuss how you can obtain pilot data, what aspects of the survey can be piloted, sample size required, and finally, what you should do if you decide to revise the survey.

There are three ways to collect pilot data. First, you can observe survey respondents responding to the survey. You could note items omitted, or pondered over for an inordinate amount of time. Respondents will often make notes in the margins–possibly valuable information. Second, you can interview pilot respondents after they have taken the survey. Alternatively, you could have them respond to a list of questions that you knew you wanted answered.

One should not think of piloting a survey as a one-shot activity. One could ask several content experts to review the items for content validity. A survey expert could review the instructions and the format of the items. A small number of respondents from the population, or one similar, could respond to the survey. Each of these piloting efforts will improve the results of your survey.

Note that in all of the above suggestions we are encouraging the use of a small number of informants. It is more crucial to get a small amount of information about several different aspects of the survey than to get a large amount of information about only one aspect. In-depth analysis of the pilot information should pay big dividends.

Finally, if the instructions or items need to be changed, one should be prepared to pilot the revised survey. Responses to the revised survey may be different from to the original survey.

Question 19. What are the piloting considerations?

The single most common way to reduce procedural error and measurement error is by piloting the research procedures. Pilot research means test running research procedures to ensure that the variables are administered consistently. Upon completion of the pilot test, researchers should have a clearly articulated and standardized set of procedures so that anyone interested in replicating the study could do so.

Wilkinson & McNeil

Although the psychologist is conducting his own interview, he should still consider piloting the interview. He needs to observe some pilot respondents to see how they are reacting to his questions. After the interview, he could ask them if they understood the intent of the questions and, if they felt comfortable in responding to the questions. Actual time of the interview should be recorded for use in the eventual consent form. It would be advisable to have a survey expert view a videotape of several interviews. (See Exhibit 13.)

Exhibit 13

Summary of Answers to the Question, "What Are the Piloting Considerations?"

Psychologist
> Observe pilot respondents.
> Ask them if they understood intent of questions.
> Note length of interview.
> Videotape for review by survey expert.

Administrator
> Have several content experts review survey items.
> Have survey expert review instructions and survey format.
> Send survey to sample of 10 superintendents in adjoining state.
> Have pilot sample respond to questions– "Any trouble understanding any of the terms?" "Were there any items that were confusing?" "How much time did it take to finish the survey?" "Any recommendations for additional items?"

Curriculum evaluator
> Have fellow evaluators in similar schools review survey.
> Call several teachers who used Old Curriculum to pilot entire phone survey.
> After pilot survey is finished, ask them what they thought of the phone survey.
> Record time of actual survey.

The administrator could have several content experts review the items and the order of the items. A survey expert could be asked to review the instructions and the survey format. The revised survey could then be sent to, say, 10 superintendents in an adjoining state. This pilot sample could be asked to respond to a list of questions, including, "Any trouble understanding any of the terms?" "Were there any items that were confusing?" "How much time did it take to finish the survey?" and "Any recommendations for additional items?"

The curriculum evaluator could have fellow evaluators in similar districts review her survey. Then she could call several teachers who used the Old Curriculum (but were not going to be in the final survey). After piloting the entire survey with these teachers, she could ask them what they thought of the phone survey. She should record how long the phone survey took.

Training of Interviewers

Phone surveys and interview surveys are labor intensive and therefore often rely on trained assistants. These assistants must be well trained in order for them to obtain data that is meaningful. Training issues span from whom you initially recruit, to procedures for training, competency standards and how you assess those standards.

If you want to obtain the survey data yourself, then the piloting is in a sense the training of the data gatherer. In such a case, the objective analysis of your interviewing would be quite valuable. A survey expert could watch you, or a videotape could be made for later viewing by the expert and yourself.

The more common situation is to hire assistants to do these routine tasks. Though the tasks are routine, they require intelligence and skill. The assistants should also be dedicated to the task. They should feel comfortable doing their job, and should have natural social graces. You have to remind yourself that not all those who apply are suited for the job, and not all that go through training can meet the standards you want.

The training process and the ultimate necessary standards should be decided at the outset. A script should be written and shared with the trainees. They must reach the criterion of a natural reading of the script if a phone survey, or memorization of the script if in-person interviewing. The trainees need to develop a smooth flow from one item to the next, and they need to do this while accurately recording the data.

The training process can include videotapes of desirable behavior, role playing microsessions, role playing among the trainees, practicing with confederates who provide the same answers to all trainees (with some responses being problematic). Finally, confederates can be interspersed with actual respondents, to verify that your assistants are continuing to provide accurate and complete data.

Question 20. What are the training considerations?

The government are very keen on amassing statistics. They collect them, add them, raise them to the nth power, take the cube root and prepare wonderful diagrams. But you must never forget that every one of those figures comes in the first instance from the village watchman, who just puts down what he damn pleases. **Comment of an English judge on the subject of Indian statistics**

The psychologist will be conducting the interviews himself, but he needs to make sure that he is internally consistent. He could videotape his pilot interviews to check on whether he asks all the questions, and all in the order intended. This would be extremely valuable as we often find it difficult to see ourselves as others see us.

The survey of school uniforms will be a mail survey, so training is less of an issue. Assistants might be hired to record the survey data, and they need to be checked to verify that they are entering the data correctly.

The curriculum evaluator also decided to conduct the phone interviews herself, and we applaud this decision as you do not want to put the outcome of your study in the hands or voice of someone else. But let us assume that the district is very large, resulting in a sample size too large for just the curriculum evaluator to phone herself. Or it may be that the evaluator decided for political or ethical reasons that she should not conduct the survey herself. Exhibit 14 contains a summary of the various responses to the training considerations.

Before she hires assistants, she needs to plan the entire training effort. She needs to develop the script to be used on the phone. She needs to plan the training format, and who will do that training. She needs to provide positive role models-preferably on videotape. She needs to train the assistants in ways to smoothly flow from one question to the next, and how to be recording the information at the same time. Some training will involve role playing of respondents by the trainees–for it is often valuable to see the process from the other side. Part of the final standard setting could involve each trainee calling the same confederate, and then comparing the taped responses. Paying a confederate to be called by each assistant throughout the actual study may not be a bad idea. Informing the assistants of this might in itself keep up the desired accuracy. Finally, the curriculum evaluator should be prepared to retrain or fire any assistant who clearly loses their passion for the job or who is providing meaningless data.

Exhibit 14

Summary of the Answers to the Question, "What Are the Training Considerations?"

Psychologist
    Piloting survey interview is in a sense a training.
    Videotape would be valuable.
    Needs to develop method to ensure all the desired questions are asked in the
same order.

Administrator
    Not applicable.

Curriculum evaluator
    Same issues as psychologist if conduct survey herself.
    But, let's assume that she decides to hire phone interviewers.
    Needs to write script for training.
    Hire dedicated and competent interviewers.
    Train to criteria of natural reading of script.
    Easy flow from one question to the other.
    Accurate recording of data.
    Train each other.
    Have each pilot teacher called by each interviewer.

Additional Reading

Question 17. What are some of the item format considerations?

Berdie, D. R., Anderson, J. F., & Niebuhr, M. A. (1986). *Questionnaires: Design and use* (2nd ed.). Metuchen, NJ: The Scarecrow Press, Inc.
    Chapter 4 includes what questions should be asked, how the questions should be asked, and what response options should be provided.

Converse, J. M., & Presser, S. (1986). *Survey questions: Handcrafting the standardized questionnaire.* Newbury Park, CA: Sage Publications
    Plenty of specific recommendations for developing your own survey.

Rossi, P. H., Wright, J. D., & Anderson, A. B. (1983). *Handbook of survey research.* New York: Academic Press.

Question 18. What are the psychometric considerations?

Committee to Develop Standards for Education and Psychological Testing (1985). *Standards for educational and psychological testing.* Washington, DC: American Psychological Association.
   Entire text deals with standards for testing.

Frey, J. H., & Oishi, S. M. (1995). *How to conduct interviews by telephone and in person.* Thousand Oaks, CA: Sage Publications.
   Discusses psychometric considerations in developing telephone and in-person surveys.

Litwin, M. S. (1995). *How to measure survey reliability and validity.* Thousand Oaks, CA: Sage Publications.
   Entire manual is devoted to discussion of topic.

Rossi, P. H., Wright, J. D., & Anderson, A. B. (1983). *Handbook of survey research.* New York: Academic Press.
   Chapter 3 discusses the measurement aspects of surveys, focusing on validity and reliability. Also introduces more technical topic of factor analysis.

Weiss, R. S. (1994). *Learning from strangers: The art and method of qualitative interview studies.* New York: The Free Press.
   Chapter 5 covers ways to improve the validity of interview data, including confidentiality issues and matching interviewers to respondents.

Wentland, E. J., & Smith, K. W. (1993). *Survey responses: An evaluation of their validity.* San Diego: Academic Press, Inc.
   Discusses accuracy levels of (a) nonthreatening topics, (b) sensitive topics, and (c) financial questions.

Question 19. What are the piloting considerations?

Foddy, W. (1993). *Constructing questions for interviews and questionnaires: Theory and practice in social research.* Cambridge, UK: Cambridge University Press.
   Good discussion on procedures to use to ensure that questions are working as intended.

Fowler, F. J. (1995). *Improving survey questions: Design and evaluation.* Thousand Oaks, CA: Sage Publications.
   Chapter 5 discusses various piloting procedures that one could use to improve the survey, including use of focus groups, intensive individual interviews, field pretesting, adapting pretest strategies to self-administered

questionnaires, and tabulating answers.

Rossi, P. H., Wright, J. D., & Anderson, A. B. (1983). *Handbook of survey research.* New York: Academic Press.
Discusses pretesting and revision of surveys (pp. 225-228).

Question 20. What are the training considerations?

Fowler, F. J. (1995). *Improving survey questions: Design and evaluation.* Thousand Oaks, CA: Sage Publications.
Chapter 7 provides a good discussion of recruitment and training of interviewers.

Rossi, P. H., Wright, J. D., & Anderson, A. B. (1983). *Handbook of survey research.* New York: Academic Press.
Chapter 9 covers interviewer selection, training, and development of training manuals.

Singleton, R., Jr., Straits, B. C., Straits, M. M., & McAllister, R. J. (1988). *Approaches to social research.* New York: Oxford University Press.
Section on field administration in Chapter 9 discusses interviewer selection and training, as well as supervision and quality control.

Weiss, R. S. (1994). *Learning from strangers: The art and method of qualitative interview studies.* New York: The Free Press.
Chapter 3 covers preparation for interviewing, including to tape or not to tape, how long the interview should be, and where the interview should be conducted.

Chapter 7

Determine the Sampling Procedure

There is a definite advantage in using as large a sample as possible. The larger the sample, the more likely it represents the population. In other words, as the sample size increases, the sampling error of the statistical results decreases. However, this is not a straight-line function. Once the population is over 30,000, the sample size needed to consider the sample representative (assuming the sampling is random) changes very, very little. For example, the sample size needed for a population of 30,000 would be approximately 380, while the sample size needed for a population of 50,000 is 381, and that needed for a population of 1,000,000 is approximately 385 (see Appendix F).

Simon (1978) identified the sample size needed for specific confidence intervals. For example, if one were interested in being 95% confident that the results of a 60%-40% split did not exceed the interval of +5, a sample size of approximately 370 would be needed. If, on the other hand, the researcher would be comfortable with an interval of +10, then a sample size of only 92 would be needed. Basically, if you want to cut the (sampling) error in half, you must quadruple the sample size. Similarly, if the sample size is cut 3/4, this only doubles the sampling error. These statements are based on a sample size of 400. As stated above, when the sample size is between 300 and 400, and the sample has been obtained randomly, it doesn't really matter how large the population is in terms of its effect on the sampling error. It does not matter if the population from which the sample was drawn was 30,000 or 1,000,000. This may not seem logical, but is an empirical fact.

Selecting the Sampling Technique

Sampling techniques can be divided into two broad categories: nonprobabilistic and probabilistic. The major difference between the two is that probabilistic sampling uses some from of random sampling procedure.

Nonprobabilistic sampling should not be used when it is possible to obtain a random (probabilistic) sample. However, usually it is unavoidable. As Kerlinger (1986) stated, some weaknesses of nonprobabilistic sampling can be lessened by replicating the study on subsequent samples.

There are three kinds of nonprobabilistic sampling: incidental, quota, and purposive. Incidental sampling generally refers to picking a sample that is convenient. It is the most frequently used sampling procedure, although the least accurate available.

Quota sampling requires prior information of the proportions of the various subgroups that make up the population of interest. The sample is then chosen to reflect those percentages. However, the individuals who are selected to represent the various subgroups are not randomly chosen. They are placed on a first-come, first-served basis.

Purposive sampling chooses respondents based on some special purpose. For example, one may want to survey a group of successful computer programmers to learn what political party they belong to and who they voted for. Based on this information, predictions can be made as to for whom they are likely to vote.

The major problem with nonprobabilistic sampling is that there is no way of determining if the sample represents the population to which one wants to infer. The major advantages are that it is usually less expensive and easier to carry out.

Probabilistic sampling is a procedure that requires a known probability of being chosen for each participant in the population. There are four basic procedures for accomplishing this, each being a modification of a procedure called simple random sampling. These four procedures are simple random sampling, systematic sampling, stratified random sampling, and cluster sampling. Before defining each of the four procedures, a brief explanation of how to use the table of random numbers will be presented.

Table of random numbers. A table of random numbers can be found in the appendix of many statistics texts. Another exceptionally good source is Rand Corporation's (1955) *A million random digits with 100,000 normal deviates.*

Most tables of random numbers consist of a series of five-digit numbers, as in Table 2. One way to use Table 2 to obtain a random sample is to assign a number to every person in the population. The researcher then arbitrarily chooses one of the columns in Table 2 as the starting point. If the researcher is interested in a sample of 30 from a population of 900, only the last three digits of the five-digit number needs to be used. For example, if Table 2 were entered at the top of the first column, the first person chosen for the sample would be the person assigned number 230 in the population. The second person would be the person assigned number 744. The number 962 in the table would have to be skipped since this number exceeds the size of the population, and therefore no one in the population would have been assigned that number. If the researcher works through one column before the 30 participants have been selected, another column would be arbitrarily chosen. This process should be continued until the desired sample size has been reached.

Simple random sampling is a procedure in which a sample of a population is drawn so that each person has an equal chance of being selected. If one used a table of random numbers as discussed above, one could then assume that each person had an equal chance of being selected. Samples chosen in such random

Table 2

Example of Part of a Table of Random Numbers

95230	30834	65975
10962	21343	79656
36744	71695	76956
13061	04222	51607

fashion are considered unbiased and representative because no one person in the population has a greater chance of being selected than any other. If the sample is not drawn randomly, then some subsets of the population may be over-represented or under-represented, thus resulting in a biased sample. Only random methods of selection allow one to assume that a sample is not biased. This is the major advantage over nonprobabilistic sampling, a procedure that does not allow this assumption.

Systematic sampling draws only the first number at random. Then every other person is drawn according to some predetermined plan, such as every ninth person. For example, if the first one selected at random is the third person, then every ninth person after the third person becomes a member of the sample, until the required sample size is met. This method is generally easier than simple random sampling, especially when a large sample or list is used.

Stratified sampling and quota sampling are very similar but differ mainly in that in quota sampling persons are drawn using random procedures to fill the quotas for each of the defined groups. When one uses stratified sampling, the population is divided into subgroups based on specific variables such as race, sex, age, economic status, or geographic location. The percentage of each of these subgroups in the entire population is maintained in the sample.

Cluster sampling defines the population as primary units of groups instead of individual people. These groups already exist, such as classrooms or regions of the state. This sampling procedure is more appropriate when it is more convenient to select groups than individuals, such as selecting classrooms rather than individuals from many classrooms. Once the clusters are defined, the sample clusters are then randomly selected. Often both cluster and stratified sampling techniques are combined to produce more representative, time saving, and economical means of obtaining a sample from the population. The major problem with the cluster procedure is that traditional statistical techniques cannot be used.

The Difference Between Random Assignment and Random Sampling

Random sampling allows one to assume that one has an unbiased sample that represents the population from which it came. Random sampling does not allow one to assume that two randomly sampled groups are the same; one can only assume that the chances have been reduced that there are differences between the two groups. Random assignment, on the other hand, uses one of the above randomization procedures to assign people to groups. Using this procedure allows one to assume that these groups are equivalent on all possible variables. But it does not allow one to assume that the groups represent the population from which they were drawn unless randomization procedures were also used to draw the sample from the population. That is, one can obtain a very nonrandom sample (such as a convenience sample) and still randomly assign all of that sample to two or more groups. Random assignment allows for distinction between groups, but only allows for generalization to the population if the sample was also randomly drawn from the population, as in Figure 1. This is an important distinction that is often overlooked.

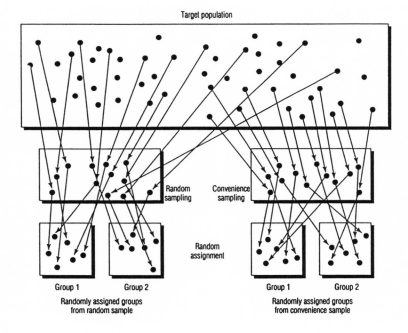

Figure 1. Comparison of random assignment under two conditions-random sampling and convenience sampling. From Wilkinson and McNeil (1996).

Question 21. How should I sample?

Oh, many a shaft at random sent
Finds mark the archer little meant!
And many a word at random spoken
May soothe, or wound, a heart that's broken!   **Sir Walter Scott**

The psychologist could conduct a probabilistic sample by:
1. Deciding to interview 50 people
2. Determining the number of telephone pages (200)
3. Decide the rate factor by dividing the pages (200) by the number of people (50) = 4
4. Randomly pick the beginning page (out of 1-4, say page 3)
5. Randomly pick position on page, say ninth name.
6. Call ninth person on page 3
   Call ninth person on page 7 (3 + 4, the rate factor)
   Call ninth person on page 11 (7 + 4, the rate factor)

This procedure would be easy to carry out, except that the call to request the interview would be time-consuming and would likely result in many refusals. The psychologist, instead, decides to put an advertisement in the paper explaining the study, what the requirements are, and what the incentive will be, along with his phone number. He realizes that his sample will consist of volunteers, some who will do anything for needed cash. But he also realizes that his future clients will be volunteers as well. He feels that the relative ease of this approach outweighs any negative aspects.

The administrator wants to survey all of the current superintendents–conducting what is called a census. She realizes that all surveys will not be returned, and that her real target population is next year's superintendents, and the superintendents in the following year. Obviously not all these superintendents exist, and some current superintendents will not be superintendents next year. Since she cannot identify particular individuals in either of these two groups, she must be content with sampling all of this year's superintendents.

The curriculum evaluator will also sample all of the sixth grade teachers who used the New Curriculum as there were few of them, approximately 20. On the other hand, since there were many more than 20 teachers who carried out the Old Curriculum, she decides to randomly sample 20 of those teachers. Such a hybrid sampling plan is not unusual. A summary of these answers appears in Exhibit 15.

Exhibit 15

Summary of the Answers to the Question, "How Should I Sample?"

Psychologist
>   Uses a convenient sample.
>   Advertises in the paper.
>   Interviews the first 50 who respond.

Administrator
>   Census sample.

Curriculum evaluator
>   Census of teachers who implemented the New Curriculum.
>   Random sample of those teachers who used the Old Curriculum.

Additional Reading

Question 21. How should I sample?

Alreck, P. L., & Settle, R. B. (1985). *The survey research handbook.* Homewood, IL: R. D. Irwin.
Chapter 3 presents additional sampling procedures of cluster sampling, quota sampling, and sequential sampling.

Rossi, P. H., Wright, J. D., & Anderson, A. B. (1983). *Handbook of survey research.* New York: Academic Press.
Chapter 2 focuses on stratified and cluster sampling. Chapter 5 is a more detailed discussion of sampling.

Singleton, R., Jr., Straits, B. C., Straits, M. M., & McAllister, R. J. (1988). *Approaches to social research.* New York: Oxford University Press.
Interesting aspect of Chapter 6 on sampling is the coverage of factors affecting choice of sampling design and factors determining sample size.

Chapter 8

Analyze the Results and Prepare the Report

The first purpose of this chapter is to sensitize the survey researcher to commonly occurring problems that make data analysis difficult or incorrect. It is hoped that knowledge of these problems will allow the researcher to avoid them in the analysis of survey data. The second purpose of this chapter is to discuss several ways of reporting the results. No matter how careful and correct you were with the previous steps of the survey, a poorly delivered report invalidates the entire survey effort.

ANALYZE THE RESULTS

To be able to competently analyze and interpret the data of a survey, one must first have clearly defined the objectives on which the research is based. In other words, the researcher must know why the survey is being conducted. The sample selection procedure should have been based on the objectives. The procedure should not have been chosen simply based on convenience, since this will make the data uninterpretable. Nonrespondents should be checked to detect if the sample that has responded to the survey is in any way different from those who did not respond. This is a crucial activity when one is interested in inferring to the population from which the sample was drawn.

One should make sure that all the data gathered and every question asked are specifically related to the objectives of the survey. Too often this is not done, resulting in confused or limited interpretation of the survey findings. It is also important to keep in mind during the data analysis that respondents have been placed in a unique situation–one that might result in their responding differently than they would have under "normal" conditions. Therefore, when one is interested in generalizing the results of a survey, it is technically accurate only when generalizing to the population from which the sample was drawn and to the specific conditions and situation under which the data were obtained. Any additional inference can only be made based on the researcher's intuition and should be clearly stated as such.

A very common error for the inexperienced researcher is the tendency to examine only one variable at a time. This limited view is likely to produce findings that are not stable; that is, they are unlikely to be replicated, or if they can be replicated, they tend to be trivial. It is generally more relevant to look at the relationship between sets of variables over time and between groups. This requires the researcher to know the content area well and to be able to hypothesize certain relationships beforehand, so that the potentially meaningful relationships will be carefully examined. This planning will maximize the likelihood that interpretable and useful results will be obtained from the investigation.

It is important that the researcher be competent in statistical analysis, and if not, the researcher should consult with someone who is. This consultation should occur before designing and collecting the data. Planning the collection and analysis of data alleviates many problems and frustrations that researchers often face. To make this consultation most productive, the researcher should have (a) clearly stated objectives, (b) specified the sampling procedure, (c) designed the data collection procedures, and (d) stated the types of questions to be answered. The researcher is then prepared to discuss these details so that the most appropriate statistical analysis can be used. The statistical consultant may at this point suggest necessary modifications to accomplish the goals of the research, thereby aiding the researcher in the design of the study and avoiding later problems.

One of the most important things to remember is that survey research is either descriptive or ex post facto. Descriptive research means that the survey is designed to simply describe the answers provided by all of the respondents. No attempt is made to compare subgroups, or to infer to the population from which the sample was drawn. If the purpose is to make that inference, then inferential statistics, such as population means, population proportions, and population standard deviations can be estimated. Ex post facto research compares two or more groups, after those groups have been formed. The researcher had no control over the formation of those groups. Comparing males to females, or volunteers to nonvolunteers are two examples of ex post facto research. In either case, the researcher does not have control of the independent variable and therefore cannot make any causal conclusions–no matter what statistical analyses were conducted. For example, if one conducted a survey and found a significant correlation between single-parent homes and juvenile delinquents, one cannot conclude that single-parent homes cause juvenile delinquency. Nor can one conclude that juvenile delinquency causes single-parent homes. Unfortunately, causal conclusions such as these are often made.

The analyses that you use depend on the stated objectives. If you want to describe the sample, then descriptive statistics such as sample size, sample mean, sample proportions, and sample standard deviation would suffice. We have found it productive to include the actual survey in an appendix with the proportion of respondents answering each item simply inserted into the survey, as in Appendix G. In this way, the reader sees (a) the actual wording of each item, (b) the various alternatives available to the respondent, (c) the proportion of respondents to each answer, and (d) the context within which the item existed. Many readers of the report will find this summary information to be sufficient.

Much additional information can be gained by comparing the responses of specified groups, such as rural-urban, respondents-nonrespondents, or male-female. These types of analyses are called "crosstabulations." Since survey research is usually ex post facto, generalizations to the desired population are strictly unwarranted. You always need to remember that the sample may be systematically different from the population to which you want to generalize, and that since groups are often formed through self-selection there are usually many differences between groups.

Inferential statistical analyses allow one to generalize to the population. Statistical analyses are often done on survey data, since there is usually interest in the population rather than in the sample that responded. One must be very careful in interpreting those inferential analyses since there are often important differences between groups other than the variable being investigated. For instance, some differences between racial-ethnic groups may be as much a function of social-economic differences. Similarly, teachers who volunteer to carry out the New Curriculum are likely to be more progressive and eager to help students in their learning than are the teachers who continue to use the Old Curriculum.

The two most common inferential statistical techniques are testing for the significant (a) correlation between two variables, and (b) difference between two means. As indicated at the beginning of this chapter, we are strong believers that multiple variables ought to be considered simultaneously, rather than just analyzing one or two at a time. Such a multiple variable approach reflects the belief that human behavior is complex and therefore requires a complex set of variables to predict and eventually understand that behavior. While one might suspect that an analysis that investigates multiple variables simultaneously might itself be very complex, that is not so. The interested reader should become familiar with the General Linear Model. (See McNeil, Newman, & Kelly (1996) for a reader-friendly approach to the General Linear Model.) The value of the General Linear Model is that the one technique encompasses all of the parametric inferential procedures that usually fill an entire introductory statistics text.

Question 22. What analyses should I perform?

The quantitative expression of social fact is to be preferred for scientific purposes whenever it can be used. It reduces individual bias to a minimum, permits verification by other investigators, reduces and at the same time makes evident the margin of error, and replaces the less exact meanings of descriptive words with the precision of mathematical notation.   **Stuart A. Rice**

The only summary information that the psychologist needs is the number of potential clients. Once he feels comfortable (as defined either beforehand or during the data collection) he can end his survey and begin to work.

The administrator will be interested in the return rate and proportion of responses for each category for each item. Furthermore, some of her objectives may have called for crosstabulations. For example, the interest in rural-urban location leads to crossing this variable with some items, such as in Table 3.

Table 3

Crosstabulation of Rural-Urban with Question 1– "School Uniforms Will Improve School Morale"

	Yes	No
Rural	0	10
Urban	40	6

Here we can see that the support for school uniforms is because of the overwhelming number of "Yes" responses by urban administrators, while rural administrators all answered "No." Without considering these two variables simultaneously, one would not have realized the different opinions of rural and urban administrators.

Another variable of interest to the administrator is that of respondents-nonrespondents. One way to identify the respondents anonymously is to include an additional postcard in your mailing with the statement "I have filled out your survey and mailed it separately. Signed _____." The cover letter would indicate that the postcard will let the researcher know who has returned the survey, without being able to link any names to specific surveys.

Much demographic data are likely available to the survey researcher, including personal data (such as sex, years of experience, and years at the district) and also data on the school district (such as socioeconomic status, rural-urban, and implementation of school uniform policy). Each of these demographic variables can be crosstabulated using the statistical technique of chi square to see if there is a significant difference between respondents and nonrespondents.

The curriculum evaluator will want to obtain sample means and sample standard deviations for each of the two groups of teachers. But because interest focuses on the implementation of the curriculum in the future, inferential statistical tests should be applied to the data. These tests will indicate if random sampling fluctuations can be ruled out as the reason for observed differences between the two means. If random sampling fluctuations can be ruled out, then the differences can be attributed to the differences in curriculum used. A test for the difference between two means would be the statistical test to be used. If the curriculum evaluator is not familiar with the test, or does not know how to do it on the computer, then the advice of a statistical consultant should be sought.

The curriculum evaluator can investigate possible differences between respondents and nonrespondents by phoning the nonrespondents. If she knows them well enough, she can ask them why they did not respond. Short of phone follow-up, she can analyze demographic differences between the respondents and nonrespondents. A summary of these analysis issues appears in Exhibit 16.

Exhibit 16

Summary of Answers to the Question, "What Analyses Should I Perform?"

Psychologist
    Number of potential clients.

Administrator
    Number of responses and proportion of responses for each item.
    Return rate.
    Perform certain crosstabulations with chi square statistic.
    Compare respondents to nonrespondents.

Curriculum evaluator
    Sample means and sample standard deviations.
    Test of difference between two means.
    May need to consult with statistician.
    Possible phone follow-up of nonrespondents.

PREPARE THE REPORT

The research report must fit the needs of the stakeholders, and therefore may be very informal or extremely formal. The major purpose of the report—communicating the results—must always be kept in mind. The more likely decisions will be made from the survey, and the more far-reaching those decisions, the more extensive the report needs to be. If this is the case, then one should include all the decisions made and the basis on which they were made.

The variety of audiences may lead to the decision to produce more than one report. The various reports could focus on different aspects of the survey, or provide different levels of detail. Technical sophistication of the audience is another factor to consider when writing the report.

Length of the report is another major consideration. Obviously, shorter reports are preferred by most readers. Often an executive summary can be of value by providing the highlights of the study for readers who are not interested in the detail.

Finally, there may be a required format of the report. We are thinking here of master's theses and doctoral dissertations that require certain information to be depicted in a structured fashion. Also, federally funded programs often require a particular reporting format. The following is a brief outline of what the report should contain:

1. Title page
2. Table of contents
3. Abstract or executive summary
4. Purpose and justification of the research
5. Review of the literature
6. Description of the methods used and the data collection procedures
7. Presentation of results
8. Discussion of results and recommendations
9. Appendices

Thesis or Dissertation Format

When the information collected is to be used for a dissertation or thesis, a very specific format should be used. While this format usually differs slightly from campus to campus, there are many similarities. It is always best to check with your advisor for clarification; however the following is what is generally accepted.

The body is usually divided into five chapters. Chapter 1 is generally entitled "Introduction." It contains a brief review of the literature to justify the need for the study. At this point you tell why what you are doing is important. It also contains a formal statement of the problem and the general research questions derived from the statement of the problem. It may end with a summary, and if you include one here, then all subsequent chapters should also include a summary.

Chapter 2 is usually entitled, "Review of the Literature." Any literature pertinent to the problem should be included. Review the most current literature first, and then work backwards chronologically. Generally you do not have to research more than 10 years. Be sure to integrate literature findings and avoid merely listing studies without showing how they are tied to the body of research.

Chapter 3 is generally entitled, "Method" or "Procedures." This chapter includes a description of the participants-who they are, where they came from; data collection procedures; description of your instrument, including reliability and validity estimates for the instruments that you will be using; and operational definitions for all variables. Restate the research questions more specifically as research hypotheses, and state the statistical method used to test each hypothesis and why that statistic was chosen. One of the most crucial parts of this chapter is a discussion of your research design (which dictates the statistics to be used).

Chapter 4 is usually entitled, "Results." This chapter states the results objectively and presents the necessary tables and figures. No discussion of the findings appears in this chapter.

Chapter 5 is usually entitled, "Discussion, Conclusions, and Implications." This chapter is the one most frequently read by someone interested in reviewing the research. Therefore, it is important to present the major findings and conclusions clearly and concisely. A brief description of what goes into this chapter is as follows:

1. A concise restatement of the problem and a summary of the basic methods and procedures.

2. A restatement of the hypotheses and the results of testing those hypotheses.

3. Conclusions summarizing and discussing the findings of the tests of hypotheses. This should be presented in detail since it is the major purpose of this chapter. It is important that the conclusions are based on the findings–one should avoid assumptions and inferences at this point.

4. Implications drawn from the findings are then presented. In this section it is appropriate to speculate.

5. Suggested applications of the findings-it is the writer's responsibility to suggest how the findings of the study can be applied.

6. Finally, suggestions are made for further research. This is the heuristic aspect of the research and should not be overlooked.

Writing a thesis or dissertation is a complex process, as so much technical information needs to be included. Furthermore, this is the first time that the person has written such a document, and usually the various committee members also need to be appeased. Appendix H contains a rating scale that can be used either by committee members or the researcher to get a feel for the adequacy of the document. A recent textbook expands on these ideas (Newman, Benz, Weis, & McNeil, 1997).

Informal Reports

When a survey has been conducted for immediate use by a particular audience, an informal written or oral report may not be sufficient. Less concern would be placed on writing style and format–more effort would be spent in communicating the results of the survey. You might even want to make a different report for each of various stakeholders, but it is usually best to report to all stakeholders.

Written report. The informal written report would have a limited literature review, and would contain the technical information in an appendix. The report would focus on the major findings and recommendations from the findings. The abstract or executive summary should be well written, as many stakeholders will focus just on that part of the report.

We have found that a technique, called the "chart essay" to be quite useful in tying together the survey objective, survey question, survey data, and recommendation. Most audiences are not interested in specific information, but instead are interested in understanding the big picture resulting from the survey. This feedback needs to be in small chunks, not unlike Sesame Street or MTV.

Graphs and pictures are often needed to entice the reader to attend to the report. One mechanism used very successfully is that of the "chart essay," developed by evaluators at the Texas A & M University. The chart essay consists of the natural language question, a brief description of the data gathering instrument, summary information, and conclusions, recommendations, or implications regarding the natural language question. If all of this information can be contained on one page, all the better. A chart essay will usually have a more technical report to back up the brief information, but most decision makers will find the chart essay to be of sufficient information.

Oral report. The oral report will rely more on informative tables and figures. The oral report needs to be short to hold the shortest attention span in the audience. It needs to be well organized, as you do not want the oral presentation to turn into many questions of clarification and confusion. Having available paper copies of the crucial tables and figures is highly recommended. Exhibit 17 compares the two presentation modes. It should be quite clear that oral and written reports require different skills, preparation, and materials.

Exhibit 17

Comparison of Two Presentation Modes

Consideration	Oral	Written
Audience?	Listeners	Readers
Formality?	Less informed	Informed
Medium?	Words & pictures	Words & pictures & & delivery
Audience attention?	Need to earn	Committed
Audience interested?	You will know	No immediate gauge
How often send message?	Once	Multiple
Interactive?	Yes	No
Who sets pace?	Presenter	Reader
Who provides advanced organizer?	Presenter	Reader can
Audience feedback?	Immediate	Delayed

Note. Adapted from Renfrow and Impara (1989).

Question 23. How should I write my report?

If it were more generally realized how much depends upon the method of presenting facts, as compared to the facts themselves, there would be a great increase in the use of the graphic methods of presentation.
Willard C. Briton

Those who write clearly have readers, those who write obscurely have commentators.   **Camus**

Since the psychologist is the one and only stakeholder, a formal report is not necessary. The psychologist should not rely on his memory of the data, since recent interviews may loom larger in his mind. In addition, it is human nature to "want to have the data turn out right." It is not in his best interest to start a business when there are not enough clients needing his specialized services. We do recommend, therefore, that data be tabled and summarized. Otherwise the basis for the decision may change; only 10% of the people interviewed are viable clients when it was decided before the survey started that at least 20% of those surveyed would have to be clients in order to decide on starting the business.

The school uniform study should report the number of surveys distributed (in this case the total population size), and the return rate. Furthermore, the proportion of responses for each alternative for each item should be included in an appendix, as we illustrated in Appendix G. Some of the most important results should also be discussed in the body of the report.

The primary stakeholders of the school uniform survey are the superintendents in the state. Since these people are usually quite busy, and may not view school uniforms as an important issue for their district, an executive summary should definitely be written and distributed to all superintendents. An example of such an executive summary is in Appendix I. The "full report" could be made available upon request and would itself be a shorter and less-technical version of the researcher's dissertation.

Evaluation reports have traditionally been extremely boring, since they tend to include all the procedures used to plan, collect, and analyze the data. Therefore the curriculum evaluator decides to use a chart essay to convey the results of her survey. Appendix J contains an example of a chart essay resulting from that fictitious curriculum evaluation.

References for Writing a Thesis or Dissertation

American Psychological Association. (1994). *Publication manual of the American Psychological Association* (4th ed.). Washington, DC: Author.

Campbell, W. G., & Ballou, S. V. (1974). *Form and style: Theses, reports, term papers.* Boston: Houghton Mifflin Company.

Newman, I., Benz, C. R., Weis, D., & McNeil, K. (1997). *Theses and dissertations: A guide to writing in the social and physical sciences.* Lanham, MD: University Press of America.

Turabian, K. L. (1973). *A manual for writers of term papers, theses, and dissertations* (4th ed.). Chicago: The University of Chicago Press.

Additional Reading

Question 22. What analyses should I perform?

Alreck, P. L., & Settle, R. B. (1985). *The survey research handbook.* Homewood, IL: R. D. Irwin.
    Chapter 9 is devoted to data processing, while Chapter 10 is devoted to statistical analysis.

Fink, A. (1995). *How to analyze survey data.* Thousand Oaks, CA: Sage.
    Entire manual is devoted to analyzing survey data.

McNeil, K., Newman, I., & Kelly, F. J. (1996). *Testing research hypotheses with the general linear model.* Carbondale, IL: Southern Illinois University Press.
    Entire text is devoted to one technique that can test almost any research question that might emanate from a survey. Authors illustrate how to use the computerized statistical package, SAS, for the analysis.

Rossi, P. H., Wright, J. D., & Anderson, A. B. (1983). *Handbook of survey research.* New York: Academic Press.
    Chapter 11 covers use of computers in analyzing survey data, including setting up the database, cleaning the data, and constructing scales. Devotes entire chapter to analyzing qualitative data. Chapter on causal modeling may be of interest to some.

Singleton, R., Jr., Straits, B. C., Straits, M. M., & McAllister, R. J. (1988). *Approaches to social research.* New York: Oxford University Press.
    Chapter 14 includes discussion on data processing of the data, including coding, editing, cleaning the data, and modifying the data.

Weiss, R. S. (1994). *Learning from strangers: The art and method of qualitative interview studies.* New York: The Free Press.
    Chapter 6 discusses issue-focused analysis, case-focused analysis, and the demonstration of causation with qualitative data.

Question 23. How should I write my report?

Alreck, P. L., & Settle, R. B. (1985). *The survey research handbook.* Homewood, IL: R. D. Irwin.

Chapter 11 is devoted to interpreting results, while Chapter 12 is devoted to report generation, specifying how each of the various item format and statistical analysis reports ought to look.

Fink, A. (1995). *How to report on surveys.* Thousand Oaks, CA: Sage Publications.

Provides details on preparing and interpreting pie charts, bar and line charts, and tables. Contains guidelines for both oral and written reports for both technical and general audiences. Provides a thorough checklist for reviewing a report for comprehensiveness and accuracy.

Newman, I., Benz, C. R., Weis, D., & McNeil, K. (1997). *Theses and dissertations: A guide to writing in the social and physical sciences.* Lanham, MD: University Press of America.

Provides examples for each chapter of a thesis or dissertation, including numerous tables and figures. Also includes several time lines for planning and executing a research study.

Pfeiffer, W. S. (1991). *Technical writing.* New York: MacMillan.

Focuses on formal reports. Includes sections on preparing charts, making oral presentations, and constructing executive summaries.

Weiss, R. S. (1994). *Learning from strangers: The art and method of qualitative interview studies.* New York: The Free Press.

Chapter 7 is devoted to writing a report based on qualitative data.

Wilkinson, W. K., & McNeil, K. (1996). *Research for the helping professions.* Pacific Grove, CA: Brooks/Cole.

Chapter 11 is devoted to publishing guidelines, including comparisons of journal article with conference presentation and master's thesis with doctoral dissertation.

References

Alreck, P. L., & Settle, R. B. (1985). *The survey research handbook.* Homewood, IL: Irwin.

Alwin, D. F. (1978). *Survey design and analysis: Current issues.* Beverly Hills, CA: Sage Publications.

Beed, T. W., & Stimson, J. (1985). *Survey interviewing: Theory and techniques.* Sydney, Australia: George Allen & Unurn.

Benz, C. R., & Hudgins, J. M. (1990, October). *Various survey formats.* Paper presented at the annual meeting of the Mid-Western Educational Research Association , Chicago.

Berdie, D. R., Anderson, J. F., & Niebuhr, M. A. (1986). *Questionnaires: Design and use* (2nd ed.). Metuchen, NJ: Scarecrow Press.

Bourque, L. B., & Fiedler, E. P. (1995). *How to conduct self-administered and mail surveys.* Thousand Oaks, CA: Sage Publications.

Committee to Develop Standards for Education and Psychological Testing. (1985). *Standards for educational and psychological testing.* Washington, DC: American Psychological Association.

Conoley, J. C., & Impara, J. C. (Eds.) (1995). *The twelfth mental measurements yearbook.* Lincoln, NE: The University of Nebraska Press.

Converse, J. M., & Presser, S. (1986). *Survey questions: Handcrafting the standardized questionnaire.* Newbury Park, CA: Sage.

Dillman, D. (1978). *Mail and telephone surveys.* New York: John Wiley & Sons.

Fink, A. (1995). *How to analyze survey data.* Thousand Oaks, CA: Sage Publications.

Fink, A. (1995). *How to report on surveys.* Thousand Oaks, CA: Sage Publications.

Fink, A. (1995). *How to sample in surveys.* Thousand Oaks, CA: Sage Publications.

Fink, A. (1995). *The survey handbook.* Thousand Oaks, CA: Sage

Publications.

Fink, A., & Oishi, S. M. (1995). *How to conduct interviews by telephone and in person.* Thousand Oaks, CA: Sage Publications.

Floyd, J., & Fowler, F. J. (1993). *Survey research methods* (2nd ed.). Thousand Oaks, CA: Sage Publications.

Foddy, W. (1993). *Constructing questions for interviews and questionnaires: Theory and practice in social research.* Cambridge, UK: Cambridge University Press.

Fowler, F. J. (1995). *Improving survey questions: Design and evaluation.* Thousand Oaks, CA: Sage Publications.

Frey, J. H., & Oishi, S. M. (1995). *How to conduct interviews by telephone and in person.* Thousand Oaks, CA: Sage Publications.

Goldman, B. A., & Osbourne, W. (1985). *Unpublished mental measurements* (Vol 4). New York: Human Sciences Press, Inc.

Goudy, W. J. (1977). *Nonresponse effect: Studies of the failure of potential respondent to reply to survey instruments.* Monticello, IL: Council of Planning Librarians.

Heberlein, T. A., & Baumgartner, R. (1978). Factors affecting response rates to mailed questionnaires: A quantitative analysis of the published literature. *American Sociological Review, 43,* 447-462.

Kerlinger, F. (1986). *Foundations of behavioral research.* New York: Holt, Rinehart & Winston.

Keyser, D. J., & Sweetland, R. C. (Eds.). (1986). *Tests: A comprehensive reference for assessment in psychology, education, and business.* Kansas City, MO: Test Corporation of America.

Krejcie, R. V., & Morgan, D. W. (1970). Determining sample size for research activity. *Educational and Psychological Measurement, 30,* 607-610.

Lavrakas, P. J. (1987). *Telephone survey methods: Sampling, selection, and supervision.* Newbury Park, CA: Sage Publications.

Litwin, M. S. (1995). *How to measure survey reliability and validity.* Thousand Oaks, CA: Sage Publications.

McNeil, K., Newman, I., & Kelly, F. J. (1996). *Testing research hypotheses with the general linear model.* Carbondale, IL: Southern Illinois University Press.

Marshall, B. G. (1976). *Mail questionnaire research: A selected bibliography with selected annotations.* Monticello, IL: Council of Planning Librarians.

Murphy, L. L., Conoley, J. C., & Impara, J. C. (1994). *Tests in print IV.* Lincoln, NE: The University of Nebraska Press.

Newman, I., Benz, C. R., Weis, D., & McNeil, K. (1997). *Theses and dissertations: A guide to writing in the social and physical sciences.* Lanham, MD: University Press of America.

Oravecz, M. T., Thomas, F., & Newman, I. (1984, October). Sample size as a function of several variables. Paper presented at the annual meeting of the Mid-Western Educational Research Association, Kansas City, MO.

Pfeiffer, W. S. (1991). *Technical writing.* New York: MacMillan.

Rand Corporation. *A million random digits with 100,000 normal deviates.* Glencoe, IL: Author.

Rea, L. M, & Parker, R. A. (1992). *Designing and conducting survey research: A comprehensive guide.* San Francisco, CA: Josey-Bass.

Renfrow, D., & Impara, J. C. (1989). Making academic presentations-effectively! *Educational Researcher, 18*(2), 20-21.

Robinson, J. P., Shaver, P. R., & Wrightsman, L. S. (1991). *Measures of personality and social psychological attitudes.* New York: Academic Press.

Rosnow, R. L., & Rosenthal, R. (1997). *People studying people: Artifacts and ethics in behavioral research.* New York: W. H. Freeman and Company.

Rossi, P. H., Wright, J. D., & Anderson, A. B. (1983). *Handbook of survey research.* New York: Academic Press.

Simon, A. H. (1978). *Basic research methods in social science: The art of empirical investigation* (2nd ed.). New York: Random House.

Singleton, R., Straits, B. C., Straits, M. M., & McAllister, R. J. (1988). *Approaches to social research.* New York: Oxford University Press.

Sudman, S., & Bradburn, N. M. (1974). *Response effects in surveys: A review and synthesis.* Chicago: Aldine Publishing Company.

Survey Research Center (1976). *Interviewer's manual.* Ann Arbor, MI: Institute for Social Research, University of Michigan.

Turabian, K. L. (1973). *A manual for writers of term papers, theses, and dissertations* (4th ed.). Chicago: The University of Chicago Press.

Weisberg, H. F., Krosnick, J. A., & Boden, B. D. (1989). *An introduction to survey research and data analysis.* Glenview, IL: Scott Foresman.

Weiss, R. S. (1994). *Learning from strangers: The art and method of qualitative interview studies.* New York: The Free Press.

Wentland, E. J., & Smith, K. W. (1993). *Survey responses: An evaluation of their validity.* San Diego: Academic Press, Inc.

Wilkinson, W., & McNeil, K. (1996). *Research for the helping professions.* Pacific Grove, CA: Brooks/Cole.

APPENDIX A

Electronic Search Engines

Boolean Basics

They are simple words, but use them correctly and you will be looking at a small number of relevant sites instead of thousands of unrelated ones. Boolean terms act as filters for finding just the information that you need. Most of the search engines on the World Wide Web–the Web–support some kind of Boolean inquiry.

The AND operator makes sure that all the terms that you request appear on the selected sites. If you type Java AND Javasoft your search will return pages about the Web's programming language, not coffee.

Use OR to return pages that contain either of the two terms.

Use NOT to ensure that certain words will not appear in the search selection.

The term NEAR finds words located within a certain number of characters of each other.

Parentheses allow you to organize your search even more by introducing order and levels, as in the mathematical use of such.

Tutorials

As in many other areas of computer software, taking time to go through a tutorial is a recommended activity. Some good tutorials are:

http://web.csd.sc.edu/bck2skol/

http://www.rs.internic.net/nic–support/roadmap96/

http:rs.internic.net/nic–support/15min/

http://oriole.umd.edu:8000/projects/Telescope/start.html

Often-Used Search Engines

http://www.dogpile.com

http://www.altavista.digital.com

http://www. metacrawler.com/index.html

http://index.opentext.net

http://www.infoseek.com

http://www.hotbot.com/

http://www.yahoo.com

http://www.mckinley.com

http://ivory.im.com/~mundie/CyberDewey/CyberDewey.html

Comparison of Search Engines

Search Engine	Ranking	Searches		
		Web	Usenet	Other Sources
AltaVista	****	Y	Y	N
Hot Bot	****	Y	N	N
Infoseek Guide	****	Y	Y	Y
Open Text Index	****	Y	N	N
Excite	***	Y	Y	Y
Lycos	***	Y	N	Y
WebCrawler	***	Y	N	N
Yahoo	***	Y	N	N

AltaVista

PROS Fast, indexes every word on millions of pages and in Usenet newsgroups.

CONS Is difficult to narrow searches.

Hot Bot

PROS Unique search options let you restrict searches in a variety of ways.

CONS Limited Boolean search features.

Infoseek Guide

PROS Searches for Web pages, Usenet groups, Web FAQs, e-mail address, and more.

CONS Uses unusual search expressions; only finds keywords.

Open Text Index

PROS Full set of Boolean search tools; indexes every word on millions of pages.

CONS Limited to five phrases per search.

Excite
> PROS Conceptual searching finds ideas related to your original terms.
> CONS Difficult to narrow searches.

Lycos
> PROS Unique search options help you speed searches and work around misspellings.
> CONS Finds only Boolean searches restricted to AND and OR.

WebCrawler
> PROS Performs reverse searches to find who is linking to your site.
> CONS Searches only by keywords; not as expansive as AltaVista or Open Text.

Yahoo
> PROS Well organized categories make it easy to drill down to useful information.
> CONS Finds only keywords.

Constraining Searches on the Web

It is possible to restrict searches to certain documents or parts of documents. Following are some options available in some search engines.

title:"The Chicago Tribune"–matches pages with the phrase "The Chicago Tribune" in the title.

anchor:click here–Matches pages with the phrase "click here" in the text of a hyperlink.

text:algol68–Matches pages that contain the word "algol68" in any part of the visible text of a page (i.e., the word is not in a link or an image).

applet:NervousText–Matches pages containing the name of the Java applet class found in an applet tag, in this case, "NervousText."

object:Marquee–Matches pages containing the name of the ActiveX object found in an object tag, in this case, "Marquee."

link:thomas.gov–Matches pages that contain at least one link to a page with the "thomas.gov" in its URL.

image:comet.jpg–Matches pages with "comet.jpg" in an image tag.

url:home.html–Matches pages with the words "home" and "html" together in the page's URL. Equivalent to url: "home html."

host:digital.com–Matches pages with the phrase "digital.com" in the host name portion of the URL.

domain:fr–Matches pages from the domain "fr." There are a few domain names: .com, .edu, .net, country codes (.fr is for France), as well as a few others.

APPENDIX B

Sample Survey Formats

[Appendix B is based on a paper presented by C. R. Benz and J. M. Hudgins at the Midwestern Educational Research Association annual meeting in Chicago, October, 1990.]

One of the most frequently attempted tasks in survey research is to measure attitudes. Attitude assessment is more difficult to obtain than factual information. A general rule is that an attitude scale should have at least 10 items for any attitude it is attempting to assess.

If a scale measuring the attitude one is interested in does not exist, then one will have to construct the instrument. Some basic scale formats used are the Likert Scale, Semantic Differential Scale, Behavioral Differential Scale, and Percentage Rating Scale. Examples of each follow. The appendix is concluded with examples of various item formats that could have been used in the school uniform study.

Likert Scale Example

On the following pages are a number of statements about which people have differing opinions. There are no right or wrong responses to any of these items. To make it easier for you to express your opinion, we have provided three degrees of agreement (on the left side) and three degrees of disagreement (on the right side). Please circle the number which best describes your opinion.

Example:
"Our system of governmental checks and balances leaves something to be desired."

strong	moderate	slight	slight	moderate	strong
+3	+2	+1	-1	-2	-3

If you disagree strongly, you would circle like this:

strong	moderate	slight	slight	moderate	strong
+3	+2	+1	-1	-2	-3

If you agree slightly, you might circle your number like this:

strong	moderate	slight	slight	moderate	strong
+3	+2	+1	-1	-2	-3

Similarly, if you agree strongly, you would circle your number like this:

strong	moderate	slight	slight	moderate	strong
+3	+2	+1	-1	-2	-3

Please be sure to make a response to each statement by circling the number that best reflects your opinion.

1. Persons receiving welfare payments should have to meet residence requirements.

strong	moderate	slight	slight	moderate	strong
+3	+2	+1	-1	-2	-3

2. All police departments should have civilian review boards to handle grievances from minority members.

strong	moderate	slight	slight	moderate	strong
+3	+2	+1	-1	-2	-3

Semantic Differential Scale Example

The purpose of this part of the survey is to measure the meanings that certain issues have for you. On each page of this booklet you will find three different issues to be judged and beneath them a set of scales. You are to rate the issues on each of these scales in order. Here is how to rate these scales:

If you feel that the concept at the top of the page is very closely related to one end of the scale, you should place your X as follows:

ISSUE: The Federal Minimum Wage Law

fair:_X_:___:___:___:___:___:___:unfair
OR
fair:___:___:___:___:___:___:_X_:unfair

If you feel that the concept is quite closely related to one or the other end of the scale (but not very), you should place your X as follows:

strong:___:_X_:___:___:___:___:___:weak
OR
strong:___:___:___:___:___:_X_:___:weak

The direction toward which you mark, of course, depends upon which of the two ends of the scale seems most characteristic of the item you are judging. If you consider the concept to be neutral on the scale, both sides of the scale equally associated with the concept, or if the scale is completely irrelevant, or unrelated to the concept, then you should place your X in the middle space:

safe:___:___:___:_X_:___:___:___:dangerous

If the concept seems only slightly related to one side as opposed to the other side (but is not really neutral), then you should place your X as follows:

active:___:___:_X_:___:___:___:passive
OR
active:___:___:___:___:_X_:___:___:passive

Work at a fairly high speed through this survey. Do not worry or puzzle over individual items. It is your first impressions, the immediate "feelings" about the items, which we want. On the other hand, please do not be careless, because we want your true impressions.

BUSSING CHILDREN TO PROMOTE INTEGRATION

fair :___:___:___:___:___:___:___: unfair
worthless :___:___:___:___:___:___:___: valuable
good :___:___:___:___:___:___:___: bad
far :___:___:___:___:___:___:___: near
active :___:___:___:___:___:___:___: passive

PRO-LIFE ORGANIZATIONS

fair :___:___:___:___:___:___:___: unfair
worthless :___:___:___:___:___:___:___: valuable
good :___:___:___:___:___:___:___: bad
far :___:___:___:___:___:___:___: near
active :___:___:___:___:___:___:___: passive

Behavioral Differential Scale Example

Every society is organized. This means that people order themselves and others with respect to other people. For instance, they feel closer to their relatives and their friends than to strangers. They feel willing to do certain things with one person but not with another.

In this part of the survey, we want to find out how you feel about other people. In the survey that follows, you will find the description of a person at the top of each page. Underneath are several statements describing things that you might do with that person. You are asked to indicate whether you consider it likely or unlikely that you would do these things with that person, if the opportunity would present itself.

If you feel that it is very likely that you would do what the statement indicates with the person, you should place an X as follows:

A COLLEGE STUDENT FAVORING NATIONAL HEALTH CARE

I would :_X_:___:___:___:___:___: I would not
talk to this person

Or, if you feel that this was highly unlikely for you to do, your answer sheet would look like this:

I would :___:___:___:___:___:_X_: I would not
talk to this person

On the other hand, if you feel that you might do this, mark like this:

I would :___:_X_:___:___:___:___: I would not
talk to this person

Or if you feel that you would be less likely to do this, you would mark as follows:

I would :___:___:___:___:_X_:___: I would not
talk to this person

The direction in which you mark will also depend upon the direction of the scale. Therefore, if you feel that you would be likely to do this, you might mark as follows:

I would not :___:___:___:___:_X_:___: I would
talk to this person

The information you provide here is confidential. The data will only be used for research purposes. Please express yourself freely in responding to the survey.

PERSON: WHITE, SAME SEX, STRONGLY FAVORS AFFIRMATIVE ACTION

I would :___:___:___:___:___:___: I would not
invite this person to my home

I would :___:___:___:___:___:___: I would not
defend this person's rights if they were jeopardized

I would :___:___:___:___:___:___: I would not
admire the ideas of this person

I would :___:___:___:___:___:___: I would not
exclude from my neighborhood

I would :___:___:___:___:___:___: I would not
take this person into my home if a riot victim

I would :___:___:___:___:___:___: I would not
participate in a discussion

I would :___:___:___:___:___:___: I would not
want as a member of my church

I would :___:___:___:___:___:___: I would not
elect this person to a political office

I would :___:___:___:___:___:___: I would not
accept as a close kin by marriage

I would :___:___:___:___:___: I would not
be alone with this person

I would :___:___:___:___:___:___: I would not
want as a roommate

Percentage Rating Scale Example

We are interested in the variation among estimations of individuals on the following items. Please circle the percentage (%) that is YOUR BEST GUESS.

1. The % of Blacks in the United States is:

0%	5%	10%	15%	20%	25%	30%
35%	40%	45%	50%	55%	60%	65%
70%	75%	80%	85%	90%	95%	100%

2. The percent of rioters in the LA riots who were unemployed was:

0%	5%	10%	15%	20%	25%	30%
35%	40%	45%	50%	55%	60%	65%
70%	75%	80%	85%	90%	95%	100%

Additional References for Measuring Attitudes

Anderson, J. F. (1986, April). *Questionnaire design and use revisited: Recent developments and issues in survey research.* Presented at the American Educational Research Association, San Francisco. (ERIC Document Reproduction Service NO ED 271 501)

Weisberg, H. F., Krosnick, J. A., & Boden, B. D. (1989). *An introduction to survey research and data analysis.* Glenview, IL: Scott Foresman.

Kerlinger, F. (1986). *Foundations of behavioral research.* New York: Holt, Rinehart & Winston.
    Provides a good, brief overview of the semantic differential technique.

Various Item Format Examples

Open-ended. Open-ended items allow respondents to indicate the detail they choose to provide. These items can provide information that would not have been expected by the developer of the survey. Summarization of open-ended questions, though, is often a high-inference activity. An example follows:

Please provide you opinions about school uniform policies:

_____
_____
_____

Dichotomous-choice. Items that divide the universe of possible answers into two categories (usually true-false or Yes-No) are called dichotomous-choice. Summary of the data is easy, though some respondents may have wished to be not as constrained in their responses. An example follows:

School uniforms will improve school morale.   Yes ___   No ___

Forced-choice. These items force the respondent to choose one of two or more options. This format should be used when the options can be viewed as equally positive or equally negative. This format is particularly valuable when respondents might likely give socially desirable responses. An example follows:

A school uniform policy will likely improve most: (check only one)
___ school morale
___ attendance
___ membership in student organizations

Scaled-choice. Also known as Likert-type items, they provide a number of alternatives on a continuum. One common continuum often used is: very positive, somewhat positive, neutral, somewhat negative, and very negative. Another widely used continuum is: strongly agree, agree, unsure, disagree, and strongly disagree. Both examples contain five options, although any number of options can be used. If an even number of options are used, then the "neutral" or "unsure" option is not available and the respondent must commit to one side or the other. An example follows:

A school uniform policy will improve school morale:

Strongly Agree	Agree	Unsure	Disagree	Strongly Disagree
___	___	___	___	___

Sociometric Questions. These questions ask the respondent to identify several people for a task or activity. The assumption is that chosen ones are more socially popular than unchosen ones. An example follows:

Suppose there was to be a meeting at which crucial decisions need to be made. List three persons whom you consider most worthy to serve as your representatives.

_____

_____

Story Identification. Provides more context for the respondent, while also forcing the respondent to choose one of the two alternatives.

ABOUT WORK AND FUN

<u>Matt Thinks</u>   <u>David Thinks</u>

Some people work too hard.   A man never works hard enough and should
They ought to spend more   always try to find more to do. He should
time having fun.   never say, "I need to have more fun."
Check one:

| I'm like Matt | I'm more like Matt than David | I'm halfway between Matt and David | I'm more like David than Matt | I''m like David |

Branching Questions. Used most often when it is anticipated that not all respondents will be able to answer a question, or if additional information is desired for a subset of the respondents. Two examples follow:

Example 1: Are you employed?   ___ Yes   ___ No

If you answered yes, please go to question question number 2 and continue. If you answered no, please go to question number 5.

Example 2: Do you participate in an HMO?
___ Yes
___ No

If no, which of the following do you have?
___ Personal M.D.
___ A group plan but not an HMO
___ no medical coverage at all
___ Other (please explain) _____

APPENDIX C

Script for the Psychologist's Interview

Have you ever had any of the following problems?

Anxiety?   never   seldom   sometimes   often

Craving to eat a lot?   yes   no

Inability to stop smoking?   yes   no

If you have had any of the above problems, do you have insurance that would cover the treatment of it?   yes   no

What insurance carrier do you have?

Did you know that you carrier covers _____ visits for the problem of _____? yes no

[If respondent does not have coverage, then ask "Would you be willing to pay $_____ to attempt to solve your problem of _____?]

APPENDIX D

School Uniform Survey

Demographic Information

School Size
_____ less than 3,000 in Your District
_____ more than 3,000 in Your District

School Uniform Policy in Your District
_____ never had one
_____ have had one for 2 years
_____ had one, but discontinued it

Survey Information

1. School uniforms will improve school morale.

Strongly Disagree	Disagree	Agree	Strongly Agree
_____	_____	_____	_____

2. School uniforms will be met with resistance from some parents.

Strongly Disagree	Disagree	Agree	Strongly Agree
_____	_____	_____	_____

3. School uniforms will decrease absenteeism.

Strongly Disagree	Disagree	Agree	Strongly Agree
_____	_____	_____	_____

4. School uniforms will decrease membership in student organizations.

Strongly Disagree	Disagree	Agree	Strongly Agree
_____	_____	_____	_____

5. School uniforms will improve academic performance.

Strongly Disagree	Disagree	Agree	Strongly Agree
_____	_____	_____	_____

6. School uniforms will have the most effect on (mark one only)
_____ Freshman   _____ Seniors

7. School uniforms will most likely (mark one only)
_____ be met with resistance by parents.
_____ have a positive effect on school climate.

APPENDIX E

Phone Survey Script

Hello, I'm Ms. Jones, and thank you for calling me at your chosen appointed time. As you know, the district is interested in evaluating the New Curriculum used by some of the sixth grade teachers this past year. As indicated in the letter sent to you, I would like to take about 10 minutes, and certainly no more than 15, to find out how you used your curriculum, and what your feelings are about it. We are obtaining this information from all the teachers who used the New Curriculum, as well as a sample of those who continued to use the Old Curriculum.

1. Which curriculum did you use this past year?
____ New   ____ Old

2. Did you and your students receive all of the necessary materials to use the curriculum?
____ yes
____ no How did that affect your implementation?
_____
_____

3. To what extent do you feel comfortable in having been trained to implement the curriculum?
____ very comfortable
____ comfortable
____ uncomfortable
____ very uncomfortable

4. How comfortable were you in implementing the curriculum?
____ very comfortable
____ comfortable
____ uncomfortable
____ very uncomfortable

5. To what extent does the curriculum match the state standards?
____ totally
____ mostly
____ some
____ little
____ not at all

6. Have you ever used another curriculum to teach math in sixth grade?

___ no

___ yes [6a. If yes, please compare that curriculum with what you used this past year in terms of helping students score well on standardized tests.]

_____

_____

6b. Which is better in terms of helping students in terms of life-long learning of math?

_____

_____

7. If you used the New Curriculum: What recommendations do you have for providing inservice to the remaining teachers in the New Curriculum, if the district decides to adopt it?

_____

_____

8. If you used the Old Curriculum: What reservations do you have about the New Curriculum?

_____

_____

9. From what you know of the Old Curriculum and the New Curriculum, which do you think is better for students in our district?

_____

_____

APPENDIX F

Population Size and Random Sample Size Needed for

Representativeness of the Population

Population	Sample	Population	Sample
15	15	650	243
50	45	750	255
65	56	850	266
80	67	950	275
100	80	1,000	279
130	98	1,100	286
150	109	1,400	303
170	119	2,000	323
190	127	2,600	336
200	133	3,500	347
210	137	6,000	362
230	145	9,000	369
300	170	15,000	376
360	187	30,000	380
420	201	50,000	381
500	218	1,000,000	385

Note. These sample sizes are for the 95% confidence level. From Simon (1978).

APPENDIX G

School Uniform Survey, with Response Data

Demographic Information

School Size

_82%_ less than 3,000 in Your District
_18%_ more than 3,000 in Your District

School Uniform Policy in Your District

_77%_ never had one
_18%_ have had one for 2 years
__5%_ had one, but discontinued it

Survey Information

1. School uniforms will improve school morale.

Strongly Disagree	Disagree	Agree	Strongly Agree
_2%__	_5%__	_77%_	_16%_

2. School uniforms will be met with resistance from some parents.

Strongly Disagree	Disagree	Agree	Strongly Agree
_15%_	_26%_	_15%_	_44%_

3. School uniforms will decrease absenteeism.

Strongly Disagree	Disagree	Agree	Strongly Agree
_ 5%__	_7%__	_70%_	_18%_

4. School uniforms will decrease membership in student organizations.

Strongly Disagree	Disagree	Agree	Strongly Agree
_25%_	_60%_	_10%_	__5%_

5. School uniforms will improve academic performance.

Strongly Disagree	Disagree	Agree	Strongly Agree
_10%_	_20%_	_40%_	_30%_

6. School uniforms will have the most effect on (mark one only)
_80%_ Freshman
_20%_ Seniors

7. School uniforms will most likely (mark one only)
_72%_ be met with resistance by parents.
_18%_ have an overall positive effect on school climate.

APPENDIX H

Rating Scale for a Dissertation or Thesis

Chapter 1: Introduction

1. Contains a good summary of the background.

    Poorly done   1   2   3   Done well

2. Contains a clear statement of the need or justification for the study.

    Poorly done   1   2   3   Done well

3. Contains a clear statement of the purpose (why the study is going to be implemented).

    Poorly done   1   2   3   Done well

4. Contains a brief but clear statement of the problem (what generated the study).

    Poorly done   1   2   3   Done well

5. Presented a good and clear set of operational definitions.

    Poorly done   1   2   3   Done well

(Same rating scale for all the remaining items, but left off to save a few trees.)

6. Research questions or general hypotheses are clearly stated.

Chapter 2: Review of the Literature

7. All the pertinent literature that relates to the problem was reviewed.

8. There is no padding.

9. All the literature reviewed was shown to be related to the specific problem.

10. Presented a good summary of Chapter 2.

Chapter 3: Method

11. Presented a comprehensive description of participants (who they were, where they came from, age, racial-ethnic identity, sex, SES, etc.).

12. Presented a clear and detailed procedure of how the data were collected.

13. Presented a good description of the instrument (why it was chosen, reliability, validity, and usability).

14. Hypotheses are clearly stated.

15. Presented the statistical methods needed to test the hypotheses.

16. Presented a clear explanation of the research design.

17. Presented a comprehensive summary of Chapter 3.

Chapter 4: Results

18. Presented the results objectively.

19. The results summarized in tables are clear and easy to read.

20. Presented a clear summary of Chapter 4.

Chapter 5: Discussion, Conclusion, and Implications

21. Presented a concise restatement of the problem.

22. Contains a concise restatement of method, focusing on the major points.

23. Presented a restatement of the hypotheses and the results for each hypothesis.

24. Presented conclusions and discussion of the findings in great detail.

25. The conclusions were based on the findings and avoided any assumptions or inferences.

26. Provided appropriate implications and inferences.

27. Presented suggested applications of the findings that are reasonable.

28. Presented suggestions for further research.

29. Presented a summary of Chapter 5.

APPENDIX I

Example Executive Summary

Executive Summary of the School Uniform Survey

Jane Doe

Anycity

(555) 555-555

The state's superintendents were surveyed in May, 1997 regarding implementation of a school uniform policy. All superintendents were sent the survey, and 90% responded. Those who did not respond were found not to be different from those who did on the variables of rural-urban, size of district, and length of service. There may be other differences that were not investigated, but it seems reasonable to assume that those responding were representative of all superintendents in the state.

Superintendents were asked to answer "Yes" or "No" to each of five items. As a group, superintendents favored a school uniform policy by a 80% to 20% margin. This was true for each of the five items, except, "School uniforms will be met with resistance from some parents," with 44% indicating "Yes." Superintendents felt that improvement of morale, decrease of absenteeism, and improvement of membership in student organizations were outcomes worth obtaining despite the resistance from some parents. Rural superintendents were not as positive about school uniform policy as were the urban superintendents. The survey is attached with percentages for each response, and separated by rural-urban. A more detailed report will be included in the next issue of the State Superintendents' Quarterly Report. The full report will be available in dissertation form from the author.

APPENDIX J

Example of a Chart Essay

Project: Evaluation of New Curriculum in Anycity

Date: September 24, 1997

Evaluator: Mary Smith, Evaluator, Anycity (555) 555-5555

Question: How do teachers feel about the New Curriculum?

Data Source: Phone survey of the 20 teachers implementing the New Curriculum and a sample of another 20 teachers from the same school who continued to implement the Old Curriculum. Responses were obtained to the following three items:

Item 1: "How do you feel about the curriculum that you implemented this past year with respect to sequencing of objectives?"

Item 2: "How do you feel about the curriculum that you implemented this past year with respect to meeting the state's competencies?"

Item 3: "How do you feel about the curriculum that you implemented this past year with respect to ease of implementation?"

The mean responses of the teachers implementing the New Curriculum (N) and the teachers implementing the Old Curriculum (O) are presented below. The scale goes from very positive to very negative.

very +   somewhat +   neutral   somewhat -   very -

Item 1: Sequencing

[_____N__O_____]

Item 2: Meets state competencies

[__N_____O_____]

Item 3: Ease of implementation

[_____O_____N_____]

Conclusion: There was no difference between the two groups of teachers using the two curricula on the sequencing item. Teachers felt that the New Curriculum covered the state's competencies better, though it was less easy to implement. Indeed, those who did implement it were "somewhat negative" about the ease of implementation.

APPENDIX K

Sample Size as a Function of Several Variables

[Appendix K is based on a paper presented by Michael T. Oravecz, Frank B. Thomas, and Isadore Newman at the Mid-Western Educational Research Association annual meeting in Kansas City, October, 1984.]

There are definite advantages to using large samples. However, researchers are frequently interested in minimizing cost and effort. In general, the more information one has, the better one is able to predict. This relationship also holds when one investigates larger samples. When one has information about the population and the desired level of confidence, one can effectively decide on an appropriate sample size.

In choosing the sample size, the usual approach is to consider the percentage result that is likely to be obtained, together with the amount of accuracy that is desired or acceptable. However, Krejcie and Morgan (1970) have shown that sample size, S, is a function of X^2, the tabled value of chi-square for one degree of freedom at the desired confidence level; P, the population proportion or percentage result likely to be obtained; d, the desired amount of accuracy around the population proportion; and N, the population size. That is,

$$S = f(X^2, P, D, N) = [X^2 NP(1-P)] \text{ e } [d^2(N-1) + X^2 P(1-P)]$$

$$= (X^2 NPQ) \text{ e } [d^2(n-1) + X^2 PQ] \quad \text{where } Q = 1 - P$$

For example, if one wished to be 95% confident that the results of a 70%-30% split did not exceed a range of +/- 5% (i.e., 65% - 35% or 75% - 25%) for a population of 15,000, a sample size of 311 would be needed. This result can be obtained from Table K-2 (95%) by finding 15,000 under the column labeled N and reading across to the column headed by .7 under the heading of d = .05.

It should be noted that if the split had been 30%-70%, the same columns would have been used since P(1-P) is the same as Q(1-Q). That is, P and Q are interchangeable in the equation and, therefore, are interchangeable in the tables.

For example, wishing to be 90% confident that for a population of 15,000 the results of 40% of the people responding in a certain way to an item did not exceed +/- 5%, one would use Table K-1 to determine the sample size needed. In this case, P = .4, Q = .6, d = .05, and N = 15,000. Using Table K-1 and finding 15,000 under the N column, and reading across to the P or Q column under d = .05 and under P or Q = .6, the researcher would find that a sample size of 256 would be needed.

From the definition of the population and an adequate listing of that population, the researcher can determine the value of N. The choice of confidence level determines the table to use and, the desired amount of accuracy specifies the value of d. However, the choice of P or Q is not left up to the researcher since, obviously, this is the result of conducting the survey. How, then, does one go about estimating the sample size needed when it varies according to the value of P or Q?

The answer is in reviewing the results of similar surveys and (not or) the results of pretesting the questions on a sample of the population. If these results do not provide clues as to which value of P to use, then a value of .5 (50%) should be selected since that value requires the largest sample size.

For example, if a researcher wished to be 99% confident that the results did not exceed a range of +/- 1% for a population of 15,000 but did not know the percentage of results likely to be obtained, he or she would use Table K-3 (the 99% confidence table) with d = .01. P = .5, and find that a sample size of 7,847 would be needed. If one were interested in less accuracy, say +/-5%, the sample size needed would be only 663.

From an inspection of Tables K-1, K-2, and K-3, it can be seen that for any confidence level, population proportion, and amount of desired accuracy, as the population increases, the necessary sample size (S) increases. However, this is not a linear relationship. As a matter of fact, it can be shown that for a given confidence level, population proportion, and desired amount of accuracy, the required sample size is a constant:

$$\text{Limit } S \atop N \rightarrow \inf} = \frac{2P(1-P)}{d^2}$$

In other words, there is a limit to the sample size needed for a given confidence level, population proportion P, and amount of desired accuracy. In the three tables this is reflected by the values across from the term "infinity," the last entry under the N column. For example, at the 90% confidence level, for a population proportion of P = .5, and a desired level of accuracy of d = .05, the sample size needed for a population of 15,000 is essentially the same as that for an infinite population; i.e., 266 versus 271 participants.

Table K-1

*90% Confidence Level for Determining Sample Size (S) for a Given Population Size (N)
for Desired Amount of Accuracy (d) for Selected Proportions (P)*

P or Q N	d = .01					d = .05				
	.5	.6	.7	.8	.9	.5	.6	.7	.8	.9
15	15	15	15	15	15	14	14	14	14	13
30	30	30	30	30	30	27	27	27	39	33
65	64	64	64	64	64	53	52	51	47	39
80	79	79	79	79	77	62	61	59	99	44
100	99	99	98	98	96	73	72	70	64	50
150	147	147	146	145	141	97	95	91	81	59
200	194	194	193	191	185	117	113	107	93	66
300	287	287	285	281	267	143	140	130	110	74
500	466	464	460	448	415	176	171	157	129	82
750	675	673	663	640	574	199	193	175	141	86
1000	871	867	851	813	709	213	207	186	148	89
2000	1544	1530	1480	1369	1099	239	230	204	160	93
3500	2308	2276	2167	1937	1438	252	242	214	165	95
6000	3182	3121	2921	2517	1734	259	249	219	169	96
9000	3966	3776	3487	2926	1919	263	253	222	170	97
15000	4667	4537	4126	3365	2098	266	256	224	171	97
infinity	6775	6504	5691	4336	2439	271	260	228	173	98

Table K-2

*95% Confidence Level for Determining Sample Size (S) for a Given Population Size (N)
for Desired Amount of Accuracy (d) for Selected Proportions (P)*

| P or Q | d = .01 | | | | | d = .05 | | | | |
N	.5	.6	.7	.8	.9	.5	.6	.7	.8	.9
15	15	15	15	15	15	14	14	14	14	14
30	30	30	30	30	30	28	28	28	27	25
65	65	65	65	65	64	56	56	54	52	44
80	79	79	79	79	78	66	66	64	61	51
100	99	99	99	98	97	80	79	77	71	58
150	148	148	148	146	144	108	107	103	93	72
200	196	196	195	194	189	132	130	124	111	82
300	291	291	289	286	276	169	166	156	135	95
500	475	474	471	462	437	217	212	196	165	108
750	696	694	686	669	616	254	247	226	179	114
1000	906	902	890	860	776	278	270	244	197	122
2000	1655	1644	1603	1509	1267	322	311	278	219	129
3500	2565	2537	2441	2230	1739	346	334	295	230	133
6000	3693	3634	3441	3036	2193	361	347	306	236	135
9000	4645	4554	4253	3652	2497	368	354	311	239	136
15000	5854	5709	5245	4359	2809	374	354	311	239	136
infinity	9600	9216	8064	6144	3456	384	368	322	246	138

Table K-3

99% Confidence Level for Determining Sample Size (S) for a Given Population Size (N)
for Desired Amount of Accuracy (d) for Selected Proportions (P)

		d = .01					d = .05			
P or Q N	.5	.6	.7	.8	.9	.5	.6	.7	.8	.9
15	15	15	15	15	15	15	15	15	15	14
30	30	30	30	30	30	29	29	29	28	27
65	65	65	65	65	64	59	59	58	46	41
80	80	80	80	80	79	71	71	70	67	60
100	99	99	99	99	98	87	87	85	81	71
150	149	149	149	148	146	122	122	118	111	92
200	198	198	198	197	194	154	152	147	136	109
300	295	295	294	292	286	207	204	195	176	133
500	485	485	483	478	461	285	280	264	230	162
750	718	716	712	701	666	352	345	320	271	181
1000	943	941	933	914	857	399	389	358	298	193
2000	1785	1777	1749	1683	1498	498	483	436	350	213
3500	2890	2869	2797	2632	2206	558	539	481	379	224
6000	4406	4357	4193	3833	2992	597	576	510	396	230
9000	5833	5749	5469	4869	3588	618	595	525	405	233
15000	7847	7722	7221	6214	4269	635	611	537	413	235
infinity	16565	15912	13923	10608	5967	663	636	557	424	239

Index

About the Authors

Isadore Newman received his PhD in educational psychology with a specialty in statistics and measurement from Southern Illinois University at Carbondale in 1971. He has been a professor at the University of Akron since 1971. During his professional career, he has served on over 300 dissertation committees and has presented hundreds of papers at state, national, and international meetings. He has written 10 books and monographs and has served on many editorial boards, in addition to being the editor of *Multiple Linear Regression Viewpoints* and the *Midwestern Educational Researcher*. He also recently published: *Qualitative-Quantitaive Research Methodology: An Interactive Continuum* and *Testing Research Hypotheses with the General Linear Model* with Southern Illinois University Press. He is the primary author on two other popular texts published by University Press of America: *Conceptual Statistics for Beginners* and Theses *and Dissertations: A Guide to Writing in the Social and Physical Sciences.*

Keith McNeil received his PhD in educational psychology from the University of Texas at Austin in 1967. He began teaching at Southern Illinois University at Carbondale that year. He ran his own consulting business for 2 years, worked in a state department of education for 1 year, worked 8 years on a federal contract providing evaluation assistance to state and local educational agencies, and worked for 5 years as an evaluator in the Dallas public schools. He rejoined higher education in 1989 at New Mexico State University, where he teaches statistics, research design, and the dissertation writing course. He recently coauthored *Research for the Helping Professions, Testing Research Hypotheses with the General Linear Model,* and *Theses and Dissertations: A Guide to Writing in the Social and Physical Sciences.*